THE RIDICULOUS PARADOX OF SUFFERING

COUNT IT ALL JOY

JOHN M. PERKINS

WITH KAREN WADDLES

MOODY PUBLISHERS

CHICAGO

All Scripture quotations, unless otherwise indicated, are taken from the Holy Bible, New International Version®, NIV®. Copyright © 1973, 1978, 1984, 2011 by Biblica, Inc.™ Used by permission of Zondervan. All rights reserved worldwide. www.zondervan.com The "NIV" and "New International Version" are trademarks registered in the United States Patent and Trademark Office by Biblica, Inc.™

Scripture quotations marked KJV are taken from the King James Version.

Scripture quotations marked (NLT) are taken from the Holy Bible, New Living Translation, copyright ©1996, 2004, 2015 by Tyndale House Foundation. Used by permission of Tyndale House Publishers, Carol Stream, Illinois 60188. All rights reserved.

Scripture quotations marked (ESV) are from the ESV® Bible (The Holy Bible, English Standard Version®), copyright © 2001 by Crossway, a publishing ministry of Good News Publishers. Used by permission. All rights reserved.

All emphasis to Scripture quotations has been added.

Edited by Elizabeth Cody Newenhuyse
Interior design: Puckett Smartt
Cover design: Erik M. Peterson
Cover image of crown copyright © 2019 by Ukki Studio / Shutterstock (1156858897). All rights reserved.
Author photo credit: Will Sterling / Sterling Photography

Library of Congress Cataloging-in-Publication Data

Names: Perkins, John, 1930- author. | Waddles, Karen, author.
Title: Count it all joy : the ridiculous paradox of suffering / John M. Perkins with Karen Waddles.
Description: Chicago : Moody Publishers, [2021] | Includes bibliographical references. | Summary: "John Perkins helps you see endurance in suffering as a virtue that makes you more like Christ and produces joy in those who trust Him. You will be encouraged to embrace suffering when it comes, stand alongside others who suffer, and believe that God will repurpose your suffering for good"-- Provided by publisher.
Identifiers: LCCN 2021017765 (print) | LCCN 2021017766 (ebook) | ISBN 9780802421753 (paperback) | ISBN 9780802499271 (ebook)
Subjects: LCSH: Suffering--Religious aspects--Christianity. | Joy--Religious aspects--Christianity. | BISAC: RELIGION / Christian Living / Devotional Journal | RELIGION / Christian Living / Social Issues
Classification: LCC BV4909 .P465 2021 (print) | LCC BV4909 (ebook) | DDC 248.8/6--dc23
LC record available at https://lccn.loc.gov/2021017765
LC ebook record available at https://lccn.loc.gov/2021017766

Originally delivered by fleets of horse-drawn wagons, the affordable paperbacks from D. L. Moody's publishing house resourced the church and served everyday people. Now, after more than 125 years of publishing and ministry, Moody Publishers' mission remains the same—even if our delivery systems have changed a bit. For more information on other books (and resources) created from a biblical perspective, go to www.moodypublishers.com or write to:

Moody Publishers
820 N. LaSalle Boulevard
Chicago, IL 60610

1 3 5 7 9 10 8 6 4 2

Printed in the United States of America

Dr. Perkins does it again. He frames suffering for us in a way that helps us not only realize and come to terms with it, but see it from a heavenly perspective, which is a hopeful one. As my wife and I have suffered much in our lives, we treasure his words in helping us to further frame the purpose of pain from God's perspective.

ERIC MASON
Founder and pastor, Epiphany Fellowship
Author of *Urban Apologetics*

I know of no one who has more exemplified joy in suffering than John Perkins. This book will be treasured by those who are hurting, those who feel as though joy seems impossible, and for everyone who loves such people. In this book, John Perkins takes the reader to Christ and Him crucified, where all joy and suffering point. Read this book and find comfort and peace and hope.

RUSSELL MOORE
President, The Ethics & Religious Liberty Commission of the Southern Baptist Convention

I'm honored to call Dr. Perkins both a role model and friend. In his own life, he has walked through suffering with deep faith and lives out what he preaches like no one else on the planet. His book *Count It All Joy* arrives right when the world needs it. We all know what it is to suffer, and in the wake of the COVID-19 pandemic, we've experienced a collective suffering like never before. In his compassionate, forthright, approachable way, Perkins reminds us that Jesus knows a thing or two about suffering, and that He loved us enough to die for us. That kind of scandalous love can be easy to forget when we're in the midst of suffering, but Perkins shows us that God can handle our soul-wrenching laments, and work all things together for our good. Whether you've experienced pain, loss, injustice, or 2020, we all need this book.

JUDAH SMITH
Lead Pastor of Churchome

John Perkins's new book, *Count It All Joy*, is a reality check for a culture gone wild for all things "feel good." He reminds us that suffering is on the menu. God's promise is that in this life we will suffer, but that He will be with us through it all. He makes it redemptive and beneficial. Our challenge is to suffer well. John Perkins shows us how.

TONY EVANS
President, The Urban Alternative
Senior Pastor, Oak Cliff Bible Fellowship

Dr. John Perkins knows suffering. He has lived a life of enduring through trials. But as he so eloquently writes in *Count It All Joy*, "None of us want suffering, but when it comes—it comes as a teacher." He has been taught by looking to our Savior, who suffered and counted it all joy. Take this journey of learning as Perkins teaches us through Scripture and life experience what it means to walk closely with the Lord and endure in this life. *Count It All Joy* is a needed word from a seasoned, wise, and godly teacher.

TRILLIA NEWBELL
Author of *Creative God, Colorful Us, A Great Cloud of Witnesses*, and *If God Is For Us*

John Perkins is a hero of mine that I'm honored enough to call a friend. His words have shown me the way forward even through the most difficult situations. But more than words, Dr. Perkins is a man of actions, living out a life of defiant love: showing what compassion looks like, for the oppressed and even his own oppressors. His story has forever changed my story.

JON FOREMAN
Switchfoot

I thank the Lord for leading my friend John Perkins to write this timely book, *Count It All Joy*. Suffering is the only power that can prevail over this world of injustice. That means we are not merely available to our Lord; we are expendable for Him. And we are happy to serve Him, whatever the cost. John Perkins believes that, and his life proves it. Now his new book will help all of us walk with him on the only path that can change the world: suffering with joy.

RAY ORTLUND
Renewal Ministries, Nashville

Whether it is suffering at the hands of others who have mistreated him in his life, the suffering that comes with self-denial, or the trials of life that have buffeted him until his ninth decade of living, Dr. Perkins has an infectious joy that comes from a place of love; that comes from God. His life and work have inspired my ministry immeasurably. Get your coffee or tea, pull up a chair, turn on the lamp, and read this book as the wisdom drips ever so generously from the pages into your hearts and minds.

DAVID ANDERSON
Author of *Gracism: The Art of Inclusion*

To Momma, Grandma Perkins, Momma Wilson,
and Uncle Bud . . . their love, sacrifices, and nurturing
shepherded me to the greatest love of all—
the love of Christ my Savior.

CONTENTS

I love Dr. Perkins and so does Transformation Church (TC). He is like our spiritual father. So much of who we are and what the Spirit of God has accomplished in us and through us to become a gospel-centered, multiethnic church stands on his shoulders. He was living what we are doing before I was born. I have so much respect for him that I dedicated my doctoral thesis to him:

To Dr. John M. Perkins,

Thank you for your unparalleled commitment to seeing the church in America break free from the dehumanizing chains of segregation and racism through the gospel. You have the marks of Christ on your body as result of living a life of reconciliation. Well done, good and faithful servant. You have fought the good fight of love. Well done.

After he taught at TC, my wife, my son, and I took him to dinner. I wanted my then- teenage son to be in Dr. Perkins's presence, to hear every ounce of wisdom he had to give. I wanted my son to one day be able to say, "My mom and dad introduced me to Dr. Perkins. I heard his stories."

While at dinner, I prompted Dr. Perkins in the right direction and the stories began to flow. He told stories of growing up in poverty as the son of a sharecropper in Mississippi; and how at seventeen years of age he left Mississippi and went to California after his older brother was murdered by the town marshal. He talked about his disdain for white people at the time, but white people in California led him to Jesus, and this led him back to Mississippi to share the gospel and to seek justice in the Civil Rights Movement. He talked about being tortured by white policemen. He talked about how far America has come in race relations, but also how far America must go. He talked and told stories and we listened.

In the midst of his legendary stories, one name and one story stood above the rest: King Jesus. Dr. Perkins loves and treasures Jesus, His gospel, and His church. He believes that Jesus not only forgives sins, but that He creates a family of different-colored skins. Dr. Perkins says, "Our churches today make reconciliation an event or an institution, rather than treating it as a gift from God and an integral part of the gospel message in general."[1]

There's the gospel magic. Reconciliation across ethnicities is not an event but a way of being in the world as God's beloved children in the Messiah. He has labored for this gospel-reality to penetrate the heart of the American church; he bears on his "body the scars that show I belong to Jesus" (Gal. 6:17 NLT). At the conclusion of his masterpiece, *One Blood*, he writes,

> Blood carries with it the idea of life, because life is in the blood. But it also carries the idea of suffering. It's this concept of suffering that I'm most aware of now. Not just suffering for the sake of suffering, but suffering coupled with joy. If we're going to make the kind of progress that we need to make with reconciliation, we have got to be willing to suffer. And we've got to be able to see joy as the end product of our suffering.[2]

As Dr. Perkins continued sharing stories, the vibe shifted when he looked at me and said, "Derwin, will you come to my funeral? I'm getting old. I'll be leaving soon." He's crying. I'm crying. We all are crying. I said, "I will, Doc."

This book is a gift. In *Count It All Joy*, Dr. Perkins is at his best, taking us by the hand and guiding us into God's grace as we suffer. The best teachers are those who have embodied the message they want to convey for long periods of time. Dr. Perkins has lived this book and now he is putting it in print to help us. I was captivated by these words: "Suffering has a way of sharpening your vision, helping you to focus on what really matters in life. It's a testing ground. I feel like God is testing me to see if I really believe the things I have been preaching all these years."

In our broken world, bad things happen because this is not yet the new heavens and new earth. If you choose to live as a person that seeks racial reconciliation through the gospel, you will suffer too. But do not be faint of heart—our suffering does not come to us empty-handed. Within it lies our healing and maturation through the gospel.

> For I consider that the sufferings of this present time are not worth comparing with the glory that is to be revealed to us." (Rom. 8:18 ESV)

DR. DERWIN L. GRAY
Transformation Church

INTRODUCTION

Now listen, you who say, "Today or tomorrow we will go
to this or that city, spend a year there, carry on business and make money."
Why, you do not even know what will happen tomorrow. What is your life?
You are a mist that appears for a little while and then vanishes.

JAMES 4:13–14

I was scheduled to speak on July 11, 2019 in Columbus, Ohio, at Xenos Christian Fellowship Church. The church has grown from a small campus Bible study to more than six thousand members. It has been my joy to work with them over the years in the development of an urban ministry where they relocated people into the most difficult, violent neighborhoods in the city. Their Summer Institute drew more than three thousand people from around the world to learn from each other. The theme for the Institute was "Christ Over All," and I was looking forward to sharing with them one more time. But God had other plans for me that day.

My flight had arrived at John Glenn Columbus International Airport the day before the Institute was to begin. Pastor Gary and Bev DeLashnutt picked me up from the airport, and we stopped at a restaurant to get something to eat before going to the hotel. I noticed a dull pain in my stomach while on the flight from Jackson to Columbus. By the time we arrived at the restaurant my stomach was hurting so bad that I was afraid to try to eat. So, we went straight to the hotel and checked in. I started getting worse and they called a good friend, Dr. Joel Gladwell. He had read my book *Let Justice Roll Down* when he was a ten-year-old boy and had decided that he wanted to use his life to help people. Years later God used him to help me get the healing I needed. His clinic is an extension of the main health service there in Columbus. They ran tests and took me by ambulance to the Ohio Health Riverside Methodist Hospital. I was there for five days.

I remember a lot of pain, a lot of morphine, and a lot of tests over those five days. It was hard for them to figure out exactly what was going on. The problem was hidden under layers of scar tissue that had grown where doctors had operated after my beating in the Brandon jail years earlier. It would be months later, while in a hospital in Jackson, Mississippi, that doctors would be able to finally diagnose all that was happening. Under all those layers of scar tissue—cancer was growing.

The doctors began to explain what I already had a sense of. This would be an extremely difficult surgery for a ninety-year-old man. There would be a lot of risks during the procedure and afterward. This would be my third bout with cancer. Twenty-five years ago, I had radical prostate cancer and underwent surgery to remove the gland. By God's grace they were able to get all the cancer. But this time would be different.

My daughter Elizabeth was with me when Dr. Gerald McKinney and the team of physicians explained how they planned to remove the tumor from my colon. Tears streamed down her face as they presented several options for getting at the cancer. Those may have been tears of gratitude that her father was receiving the best medical care, or they may have been tears of concern about what was to come. I'm not sure, but I was so grateful that the best medical minds in the state of Mississippi had come together to plan how to deal with the cancer. There were days with more questions than answers, but I was trusting the Lord to help them do what was best.

Anyone who has had surgery knows that the hardest part for the patient is after doctors close up the wound and you come off the anesthesia. My surgeon told me that they had to be careful with the medicine. There is a thin line between giving too much and not enough. Too much will kill you. Not enough causes you to suffer. For me that was when the dark night of the soul carried me away in a kind of pain and agony that I had never experienced before. I don't have words for that kind of pain. I was told that a lot of what I said did not make sense. When the pain was at its worst and I could no longer bear it, everything went dark. It got quiet and I was in a coma—how long, I don't know. I woke up just briefly and went back into a deep, deep sleep for hours.

When I finally woke up, the pain was still there, but I noticed something else. I felt a different sense of peace. It's hard to explain and put into words. During my time of deep sleep, I dreamed of blocks that all had the word "meaning" printed on every side. And I felt the presence of the Lord. I finally understood that all of life is wrapped up in Him. When He said that He had come that we might have abundant life, that abundant life is a meaningful life, full of His presence.

There's an old gospel song that suggests that if we want to have a home in heaven we need to send up the timber for the building.

There's a dream that I dream,

Of my heavenly home,

I know that I'm going there one day, yes I am.

Maybe morning, night or noon
I don't know just how soon,
That's why I'm sending up my timber every day.[1]

When I woke up, I said to my daughters, "I finally found what I was longing for!" I've had a sense of longing for just about all my life. I felt like God was letting me know that I didn't need to send up any more timber. I could finally rest.

I believe that deep down in all of us we have this idea that we can add something more to our own redemption—our own good works. Henry Cloud and John Townsend wrote, "This is the law working within us. It helps some very sick parts of us—such as our self-righteousness, our pride, and our fear of being dependent—feel safe, in control, and less vulnerable and needy."[2]

For much of my life I have felt like I had to keep going, keep running, and keep doing more and more for God to be pleased with me. But that's a works-based salvation. Our salvation was bought with the precious blood of Jesus, not by anything we do. I *know* that in my head. I know that the apostle Paul said, "For it is by grace you have been saved, through faith—and this is not from yourselves, it is the gift of God—not by works, so that no one can boast" (Eph. 2:8–9). I know that we are chosen. We are called. But I still felt like I had to do something more.

After all these years, and while in deep sleep after the surgery, I finally sensed the Lord saying to me, "John, stop working for your redemption. I have gone to prepare a place for you. *Everything* is done. *Everything is ready.*" So, I am finally at peace: I don't have to strive and work to do something more so that God will be pleased with me. My soul is satisfied. And I'm grateful for that. So very grateful.

When I was able to go back to the New Horizons Church after the surgery, it seemed like the message was meant for me. My pastor, Rev. Dr. Ron Crudup, preached from the apostle Paul's message to the Philippian church. Paul talked about his thanksgiving for the Philippian church: "I am torn between the two: I desire to depart and be with Christ, which is better by far; but it is more necessary for you that I remain in the body" (Phil. 1:23–24). I understood what Paul meant when he said that he was ready to be with the Lord. I believe in my heart that to live is Christ and to die is gain, and I felt at peace with the expectation of heaven and the joy of being with Him. I think that's the joy that the Lord gives us even in times of suffering. It's the kind of joy that reminds us that "trouble don't last always."

This journey with cancer has helped me see a lot of things more clearly. Suffering has a way of sharpening your vision, helping you to focus on what really matters in life. It's a testing ground. I feel like God has been testing me to see if I really believe the things I have been preaching all these years. The Scripture I have been quoting for so long, do I really believe it? I've had to wrestle with that. I'm asking the Lord to give me a little more time to write this message. There are things I want to say that I have not been able to say before.

> **I FEEL LIKE GOD HAS BEEN TESTING ME TO SEE IF I REALLY BELIEVE THE THINGS I HAVE BEEN PREACHING ALL THESE YEARS.**

When I wrote *One Blood: Parting Words to the Church on Race and Love*, my heart was torn to see God's church so divided along the lines of race. How His heart must grieve to see the ones He shed His blood for refuse to worship Him together. We see color first, and it blinds us to His image in each of us. I concluded that book by saying:

> The Church must speak out with one voice against bigotry and racism. We have been too quiet. The time is now. A platform has been placed in front of us and we must speak with clarity and truth. We've made a mess of things, but there is a path forward. It will require us to hold fast to His vision for one Church and the biblical truth of one race. We need to lament our broken past and be willing to make some personal confessions about our own part in this [sinful] mess. Then we'll have to be willing to forgive and move forward toward true repentance. We must be committed to the fight until the battle for reconciliation is won. And we must never forget that our power is not in guns, weapons, or armies. Our power is on our knees before our God.[3]

I believe this more than ever with the killing of George Floyd. The nation watched in shocked silence as the life of this black man ebbed away for more than eight minutes under the knee of an officer of the law who was sworn to protect the community. Our nation is suffering an integrity crisis after generations of neglect on the reconciliation front. We need to pray as never before—and then we need to get up and act.

As I have traveled across the country, people constantly asked me how to put the message of *One Blood* into action. They needed some action steps for living out the message of biblical oneness. And that's why I wrote *He Calls Me Friend: The Healing Power of Friendship in a Lonely World*. I believe that friendship is the way over and through the hard lines of race, class, and gender that have separated us from one another. God Himself shows us the pattern for biblical friendship as the Hound of Heaven follows hard after us, waiting on us to turn to Him, forgiving our sins, and promising to never leave us. Friendship is Christian discipleship. It's the outliving of the inliving Christ. God has chosen to make us His friends and expects us to pursue others for friendship—just like He has done for us. We are to live for Him and make Him known.

The messages of *One Blood* and *He Calls Me Friend* are not easy messages to put into practice. They require sacrifice—and in some cases real suffering. It will cost something to cross lines that you've never crossed before. It will cost something to admit that you have held wrong thoughts about other people just because they don't look like you. You will surely have to die to yourself in order to do that. You will need to willingly sacrifice wrong notions about the worth and value of other people. This dying to self—a daily death—is what we are called to.

IT WILL COST SOMETHING TO CROSS LINES YOU'VE NEVER CROSSED BEFORE.

That's asking a lot in a day and time when sacrifice and suffering are such unpopular messages. It seems like our world has been carried away with the ideas of success, happiness, wealth, and fame. Even the Puritans' prayers spoke of this desire for the easy life: "They earnestly desire and eagerly pursue the riches, honors, pleasures of this life, as if they supposed that wealth, greatness, merriment, could make their immortal souls happy; But, alas, what false delusive dreams are these!"[4] Much time has passed, but some things have remained the same. We still want the easy life. No one wants suffering; it's an unwelcome visitor.

None of us want suffering, but when it comes—it comes as a teacher. Suffering continues to teach me even at this stage of life. I haven't always cooperated with the lessons, but the Lord has a way of getting my attention and making the lesson plain. There are many kinds of suffering, but in this book I want to talk about two distinct and very different kinds of suffering. First, there's suffering that chooses you, like the suffering of Job that we're all so familiar with. It's suffering that has your name on it and it doesn't have anything to do with something you did to deserve it. It comes unexpectedly and can shake the foundations of your life. It can drive you to your knees, or it can make you want to curse God.

When I look back over my life, I see a lot of that kind of suffering. My mother died of starvation when I was only seven months old. My brother was murdered when I was sixteen years old. My oldest sister was killed by her boyfriend. And two of my sons died way before I was ready to let them go. I'll talk about lessons from this kind of suffering in **Part One** of this book.

And then there's the suffering that you choose. We'll look at this in **Part Two**. It's when you choose to die to self and pour out your life as an offering to the Lord, like so many of the New Testament saints did. I want to lift up suffering as a worthy offering to our Lord, who showed us how to suffer well. This is what it will take for us to cross the hard racial divides and love one another.

When I went to the Rankin County Jail in Brandon, Mississippi to visit nineteen Tougaloo College students who had been arrested after a protest march on February 7, 1970, I knew there was the possibility of being arrested. I knew all about the dangers of racism in the heart of Mississippi. But I didn't expect the level of torture that I experienced at the hands of the sheriff in the Brandon, Mississippi, jail and the Mississippi Highway Patrol.

Those were the costs that many civil rights workers paid to turn the tide toward equality for all people. We're seeing people who are learning about the high cost of reconciliation today, as marchers and protesters circle the globe. Many have been beaten; others thrown in jail. William Cullen Bryant said, "Truth crushed to earth will rise again."[5]

I see truth rising today. There's an old hymn that asks, "Must Jesus bear the cross alone, and all the world go free?" The hymn writer answered his own question by saying, "No, there's a cross for everyone and there's a cross for me." I believe that.

Even as I am in the grip of suffering at this moment, I know this to be true: that even as this body is wasting away, my inner man is being renewed every day. And I am comforted in knowing that, as the apostle Paul said, "our present sufferings are not worth comparing with the glory that will be revealed in us" (Rom. 8:18).

The first-century church had a good handle on suffering. For many of them, to name the name of Christ meant being sent to Nero's chopping block. It meant almost certain imprisonment and death. For many believers around the world today that is still the case. There are still places where it costs your life to name the name of Jesus. Voice of the Martyrs is an organization that works to tell the stories of people who are persecuted for their faith around the world. We can be grateful that's not the case in America. We're not there yet. But there's a shifting that's happening. We're turning away from principles that are rooted in Scripture. Some scholars who are futurists say that the tribalism they are seeing in our country could easily lead to genocide. The signs are already there. When armed militia threaten the lives of governors they disagree with, and there is encouragement to fight rather than to reason with one another, we're heading into dangerous territory. The day may come soon when we will all need to be prepared to suffer for our faith. The church will need to know how to suffer well.

That's true for the church, but it's also true for every one of us. The enemy of our souls wants nothing more than to be able to sift us and shred our faith right now. His desire is to shake the foundations of your faith and cause you to walk away, convinced that Jesus is not strong enough to carry you through. I don't know how he's sifting you right now. He seems to be sifting the entire world with the COVID-19 pandemic. As I write this, many of us are caught in the grip of fear and suffering from a virus that seems to be out of control.

You may be dealing with your own battle with cancer or some other serious disease. Maybe it's the death of someone you loved dearly, a marriage that's crumbling, financial collapse, or betrayal by a trusted friend. Suffering comes in so many forms. And if God's Word is true, it will enter and affect each one of our lives in some way or another. Life is full of it.

So, this book is about suffering. But it's not just about suffering. It's about the *paradox* of suffering. The word *paradox* is from the Greek *paradoxon*, which means "contrary to expectations, existing belief, or perceived opinion."[6] A paradox is when you get what you don't expect. You don't expect to find joy when you're suffering. **Part Three** will cover this paradox of joy. I'm finding out that it is possible to have joy right in the middle of suffering. Joy is a deep feeling of knowing that everything is going to be all right—no matter how bad things seem to be.

I looked at my wife, Vera Mae, the other day, and we both smiled at the thought of finishing well and knowing that heaven is waiting on us. I think back to eighteen years ago when it looked like the Lord was ready to call her home. I pleaded with Him to allow her to live so that she could help me finish the work He's given me to do. He did that. Now we're both ready to be offered up—whenever He's ready for us. We will soon get to hear His "well done." That's joy right in the midst of some serious realities.

I've recently begun a course of treatments that will likely extend to the end of my life. Vera Mae and I will see cancer as the last fight of our lives. She has lost her vision, the ability to walk, and just recently had to have a toe amputated. For these last eighteen years she has been holding me up and giving me strength to carry on. And through it all, we're holding on to our joy. We have the joy of the Lord. We have the joy of friends and family. We have the joy of the church. We rejoice in all of this.

Only God can put suffering together with joy and make it make sense. From this vantage point I can say that there is a deep, deep kind of intimacy with my Lord that I had not achieved until just now. It has taken cancer for me to be able to feel His favor and His pleasure. And in that I find great joy. Joy unspeakable. It does not erase the reality of the pain or the intensity of the struggle. But it is a joy that carries me. It soothes me to sleep at night and wakes me early every morning thankful for another day. So, I keep serving Him, sometimes through tears, sometimes with anguish of heart. There's a gospel hymn that says, "I don't feel no ways tired." The truth is that I am getting tired. My steps are getting slower. But the rest of that song says, "I've come too far from where I started from / Nobody told me that the road would be easy / I don't believe He brought me this far to leave me."[7] To that I can say, Amen.

Charles Spurgeon said, "I am certain that I never did grow in grace one-half so much anywhere as I have upon the bed of pain."[8] And again I say, Amen. This is the message that I want to leave as a witness to the next generation: It's not only given that we should believe on God, but that we should suffer for His namesake. Let's talk about the lessons of suffering and joy . . .

Nobody told me that the road would be easy
I don't believe He brought me this far to leave me.

Two Gardens and Suffering

Now the LORD God had planted a garden in the east, in Eden;
and there he put the man he had formed.
GENESIS 2:8

Then Jesus went with his disciples to a place called Gethsemane,
and he said to them, "Sit here while I go over there and pray."
MATTHEW 26:36

I've been thinking a lot about the question of where suffering came from. For as long as I have lived I've been surrounded by suffering. Being born to a poor black woman in the Jim Crow South was just the beginning of a life of suffering. I have suffered the loss of my brother, and two of my sons. I've suffered physical pain and torture and repeated visits with the arrows of cancer. But I am not alone in this. Suffering is everywhere.

With the arrival of the coronavirus we are experiencing suffering around the world in a way that has never happened before. From China, to Japan, Korea, Europe, South America, to the

United States—there is mass suffering. The young and the elderly are dying. People are suffering the loss of employment and are struggling to survive like we struggled during the Great Depression. I never thought that I'd see food lines like this all over the country again. People who have never had to ask for help before are finding it necessary to just feed their families . . . suffering.

Suffering is everywhere . . . but where did it come from?

IT STARTED IN THE GARDEN

When I read my Bible, I see God creating a perfect world for the first man and the first woman. Life in the Garden of Eden must have been awesome. It was full of happiness and joy every day. The garden was abundant with trees that they could eat from. "The LORD God made all kinds of trees grow out of the ground—trees that were pleasing to the eye and good for food" (Gen. 2:9a). I imagine it was God's intention for people to live like that always, enjoying life and having fellowship with Him. But Genesis 3 records a conversation between Eve and the serpent that changed everything. He tempted her to question God's goodness and God's heart for her. She gave in to the temptation, drawing Adam along.

The first sign that something was wrong was when God came into the garden after they had eaten of the forbidden fruit. He had been coming into the garden in the cool of the day and having fellowship with them. Now the Lord returns, and they've gone into hiding. He calls out to Adam, "Where are you, Adam?" Adam was hiding because he was afraid. He realized that he was naked. Fear was the first consequence of the fall, and it is deadly.

I think fear is like psychological torture. That's a special kind of suffering. It has had me in its grips so many times. I've found that only one or two percent of my fears ever come to pass—but the soul damage is done still.

Fear damages our trust and challenges what we really believe. During the Great Depression the whole nation was overcome with fear—just like so many of us are today. Many ran to the banks and withdrew all their money. President Franklin Delano Roosevelt's response has become a classic: "the only thing we have to fear is fear itself."[1] He went on to challenge everyone to stay away from "nameless, unreasoning, unjustified terror which paralyzes."[2] Fear does paralyze. And it can get the best of us, especially when we suffer. And it all started in the garden . . . and so did death.

Death followed close on the heels of Adam and Eve's disobedience to God. He had commanded them not to eat from the tree of knowledge of good and evil: "but you must not eat from the tree of the knowledge of good and evil, for when you eat from it you will certainly die" (Gen. 2:17). They did not die right away, but the process of death began. Adam lived for 930 years—but he died. And their immediate suffering took on a variety of forms. Eve would endure pain when giving birth; Adam would have to toil to produce food after God cursed the ground; and men and women would work against each other rather than with each other. The hardest consequence was that they lost the face-to-face fellowship with God when they were put out of the perfect garden that He had prepared for them.

That's a lot of suffering. The very first suffering known to mankind was because of sin. The first suffering came from knowing that they were broken. And from that brokenness—that all of us are born into—all manner of sin and suffering has come

> **I NEVER THOUGHT I'D SEE FOOD LINES ALL OVER THE COUNTRY AGAIN.**

forth. I want to rush to say that a whole lot of the suffering that we will talk about here has nothing to do with our own sin, but in the beginning that's what got it all started. They disobeyed God's command, sin came into the world, and suffering was the consequence. All of sin is represented by "the lust of the flesh and the lust of the eyes, and the pride of life" (1 John 2:16 KJV). And I think we can pretty much say that when we disobey God's command we may suffer as a consequence.

The suffering that began in the Garden of Eden has been multiplied over and over again throughout the generations. God told Adam and Eve about how they would suffer because of their disobedience. There had to be consequences for sin. But He also spoke about how He intended to fix things. "And I will put enmity between you and the woman, and between your offspring and hers; he will crush your head, and you will strike his heel" (Gen. 3:15).

HELP FOR OUR SUFFERING

We know that he was talking about the God-Man who would come to earth to fix the sin problem. The Old Testament prophets spoke of His coming and what He would do: "Surely he took up our pain and bore our suffering, yet we considered him punished by God, stricken by him, and afflicted. But he was pierced for our transgressions, he was crushed for our iniquities; the punishment that brought us peace was on him, and by his wounds we are healed. We all, like sheep, have gone astray, each of us has turned to our own way; and the Lord has laid on him the iniquity of us all" (Isa. 53:4–6). This is the glorious gospel! God the Son came to suffer for our sin and to die for us. All of us are sinners and desperately need that wonderful news. If you're reading this book and you've never asked Him to be your Savior, I beg you to do that. You can pray a very simple prayer: "Lord, I am a sinner. I believe that You died for my sins, and that You offer me eternal life. I accept You as my Savior. Please show me how to live for You." If you prayed that prayer sincerely, you are now a child of God. Jesus is your Savior, and He will show you how to live for Him.

Jesus lived without sin, and at the end of His earthly life we find Him in another garden—the Garden of Gethsemane—before He was taken away and crucified. "Gethsemane means 'oil press,'" and it "was located at the foot of the Mount of Olives,"[3] outside of the walls that enclosed and protected Jerusalem. The pressure that Jesus was under on that night in Gethsemane was unspeakable. Sweat dripped like great drops of blood as He was squeezed like an olive in an oil press. He was in agony as He drew His disciples into His suffering, asking them to pray for Him. His soul was burdened and overwhelmed with sorrow. This was the garden where sin and suffering met their match. Jesus, knowing all that was to come, declared, "Yet not as I will, but as you will" (Matt. 26:39c), as He submitted to His Father's plan and paid the price for our sin. What happened in the first garden is being reversed in the second garden. Disobedience reigned in the first garden. Obedience reigned in the second garden.

TWO GARDENS

The Garden of Eden and the Garden of Gethsemane. In the first garden we see the love of God as He prepared a perfect place for Adam and Eve to live. And we see the wrath of God as He judged their sin and disobedience. In the second garden we see the love of God as He suffered and prepared to die to satisfy His own requirement for the atonement of sin. And we see God's wrath as He prepared to lay all our sins on Jesus.

These two gardens have taught me two very important lessons that have colored and seasoned how I view suffering in my own life. They remind me that my Lord knows something about suffering. He knows deeply about suffering, because His whole earthly life was wrapped up in suffering. After He began His ministry He had no place to call His home. He was rejected by the people He came to save and betrayed by the ones He chose as His disciples. He suffered an agonizing death on the cross for my sins. He knows about suffering.

When I watched the movie *The Passion of the Christ*, I flinched every time the whip lashed His back. I couldn't bear to watch them nail the spikes into His feet and hands. He knows. He knows suffering. He sees our suffering and He rushes to us. I love that song "No, Never Alone." It reminds me of His promise to never leave me alone. I need to remember that He is with me when I suffer. And I take comfort in knowing that He knows just how much I can bear.

Some people think that God won't put more on you than you can endure. I'm not sure I agree with that. I believe that He *does* put more on us than we can handle. If I could handle it all on my own I wouldn't need Him. But because the burden is so heavy, it makes me cry out to Him. And when I cry out to Him, He meets me right there in the place of my pain. And He feels what I feel. He hurts when I hurt. I believe that.

And these two gardens teach me something else. They teach

me that He loves me. He loved me enough to die for me. I don't know any other person who would do that. He died for me. He loves me. Suffering has a way of making you forget this one important truth. You can spend a lot of time in sorrow's valley feeling like God has forgotten about you and doesn't care. I love the words of J. I. Packer in *Knowing God*: "What matters supremely . . . is not . . . the fact that I know God, but the larger fact which underlies it—that He knows me. I am graven on the palms of His hands. I am never out of His mind. . . . He knows me as a friend, one who loves me; and there is no moment when His eye is off me, or His attention distracted from me, and no moment, therefore, when His care falters. There is unspeakable comfort . . . in knowing that God is constantly taking knowledge of me in love and watching over me for my good."[4] Oh, how I need to remember that when I'm in sorrow's valley.

> **HE WAS IN AGONY AS HE DREW HIS DISCIPLES INTO HIS SUFFERING, ASKING THEM TO PRAY FOR HIM.**

The Garden of Gethsemane and the cross remind me of His care. Both gardens help me see suffering a little differently. I must somehow fit together in my mind the reality of my suffering with the truth that He loves me. My suffering is real. So is His love. He loves me. All of this helps prepare my heart for when suffering chooses me.

The words of this simple children's song ring in my heart and cover me when I hurt the most: "Yes, Jesus loves me . . . for the Bible tells me so!"

A good friend tells me that when she was growing up in Kansas they would often be struck by tornadoes that swooped down from Topeka to Kansas City. This area was known as Tornado Alley, and they were the worst at nighttime. When the tornado alarms went off, her mother would hurry around unplugging every electrical device in the house. She would turn all the lights out. They would sit perfectly still in their living room while the storm passed overhead, because her mother said, "Be still . . . listen . . . God is speaking." In the storm, God was speaking. When we suffer, it's a lot like that. Sometimes we just have to be still and hear what God is saying. There's a lot of suffering going on in our country right now. We're in the midst of a dark, dark storm of a pandemic and racial strife. People are hurting. We've already had to unplug from a lot of our usual activities. Many of us have sheltered in place. God has caused us to be still. God is speaking. Let's be still. Let's listen for His still, small voice.

> God's love is not content to leave us in our weakness, and for this reason he takes us into a dark night. He weans us from all of the pleasures by giving us dry times and inward darkness. . . . No soul will ever grow deep in the spiritual life unless God works passively in that soul by means of the dark night.[5]

PART ONE

WHEN
SUFFERING
CHOOSES YOU

CHAPTER ONE

Chosen to Suffer

"Then the LORD said to Satan, 'Have you considered my servant Job?
There is no one on earth like him; he is blameless and upright,
a man who fears God and shuns evil.'"

JOB 1:8

I believe that God chose me to be a Bible teacher. There's nothing that I love more than sitting down with the Word and speaking of His goodness. I believe that He chose me to be a husband and father. Joy overflows when I think about His kindness in allowing me to be married to Vera Mae for more than seventy years and to be the father of our children. To be the head of our family. I love being chosen by God for these wonderful experiences. But the story of Job helps me get my head around another truth: the same God who chose me for blessings can also choose me for suffering.

RIGHTEOUS JOB

Job was a good man. He was so good that God bragged on him. God told Satan that there was no one as righteous as Job in the whole earth. Have you ever wondered what God says to Satan about you? Can He say that you are upright, that you fear Him, and you turn away from evil? He said that about Job. We get to see a little of what that looked like, as Job made sacrifices for his children. He made sacrifices to God just in case his children had sinned and had "cursed God in their hearts" (Job 1:5). And Job did this continually, because his children seemed to have a party going on every day.

> **HAVE YOU EVER WONDERED WHAT GOD SAYS TO SATAN ABOUT YOU? CAN HE SAY THAT YOU ARE UPRIGHT, THAT YOU FEAR HIM, AND YOU TURN AWAY FROM EVIL?**

Job wasn't perfect, but he was good. And it was expected that he would be blessed. And Job *was* really blessed. He had thousands of sheep and camels, hundreds of oxen and female donkeys. He had seven sons and three daughters who all were doing well. Job was a wealthy man. I think maybe that's what made Job so special. He wasn't just godly. He was rich *and* godly. He had not allowed his wealth to make him forget God. He was so zealous to please God that he even anticipated that his children might have done something to offend God. He was doing everything he knew to do to serve and worship God.

BLESSING FOR OBEDIENCE, PUNISHMENT FOR SIN

It is believed that Job lived during the time of Abraham's early ancestors and long before the nation of Israel was formed. *The Moody Bible Commentary* suggests that there was a body of oral truth that was passed on from generation to generation from the time of Adam and Eve.[1] Job's theology about God would have come from this. And based on how his friends kept pushing him to admit to whatever sin had caused his misfortune, there was among the people an expectation of blessings for being good, and judgment for mistreating others and taking advantage of the poor. It is reassuring to know that some of the earliest writings in God's Word wrestle with the "why do we suffer" question.

This idea was brought forward in God's covenant with Israel much later. When they obeyed Him, He blessed them. If they disobeyed, they were subject to His judgment. As Moses prepared them to go into the promised land he reminded them, "If you fully obey the LORD your God and carefully follow all his commands I give you today, the LORD your God will set you high above all the nations on earth. All these blessings will come on you and accompany you if you obey the LORD your God: You will be blessed in the city and blessed in the country. The fruit of your womb will be blessed, and the crops of your land and the young of your livestock—the calves of your herds and the lambs of your flocks. Your basket and your kneading trough will be blessed. You will be blessed when you come in and blessed when you go out" (Deut. 28:1–6).

But if the people chose to disobey, there were warnings. "However, if you do not obey the LORD your God and do not carefully follow all his commands and decrees I am giving you today, all these curses will come on you and overtake you: You will be cursed in the city and cursed in the country. Your basket and your kneading trough will be cursed. The fruit of your womb will be cursed, and the crops of your land, and the calves of your herds and the lambs of your flocks. You will be cursed when you come in and cursed when you go out" (Deut. 28:15–19).

This idea of blessings for obedience and judgment for disobedience is seen again in the New Testament when Jesus healed a man who had been blind since birth. The disciples asked Jesus who had sinned to cause the man to be born blind. They wondered if he had sinned in the womb or if he was blind because of his parents' sin. Jesus blew their minds when He told them that the man's blindness had nothing to do with anybody's sin—it was to allow God's power to be made known.

> WE DARE NOT LOOK AT SOMEONE ELSE'S SUFFERING AND DECIDE THAT THEY ARE BEING PUNISHED FOR THEIR SIN.

And still today, when we suffer we often feel like God is punishing us or is angry with us about something. When we suffer, this is where the enemy steps in. He brings condemnation and doubt. He makes us question whether we really do belong to the Lord. We need to be careful about allowing him to distract us from what is really going on. The story of Job tells us that we cannot always draw a straight line from suffering to sin. We dare not look at someone else's suffering and decide that they are being punished for their sin.

IT'S HIS STORY

I've read the story of Job again and again for many years. And I'm convinced that his story is not really about him at all. The story of Job is not about Job. It's not about his friends. It's not about his wife. (A lot has been said about her telling him to curse God and die. But it's not about her.) The story of Job is about God. We need to keep our eyes on Him throughout the story of Job to see what

He is doing. Job is responding, but God is initiating. Job's friends are judging, but God is adjusting the limits of Job's suffering—enlarging the boundaries that Satan can operate within. God actually suggests Job to Satan. However, it's important to note that Satan is not a major player in Job's story. In his commentary on Job, Francis Andersen argues the point strongly that Satan's role in the story line is minor. "His place in its theology is even less."[2] And he reminds us that Satan doesn't show up at all after Job 2:7.

I love how Paul Tripp speaks of this in his book *Suffering*: "We don't live under the sovereign control of the forces of evil. We live in a world that's been terribly broken by sin but still sits under the power and authority of the One who created it. You may not see his hand, and it may be very hard to accept that what you've had to endure has come under God's watch, but Scripture is clear about the nature and extent of his rule. The fact that God is in control tells us that there's divine reason and purpose to all we face."[3]

God tells Satan just how he can attack Job. God tells Satan he can go even further, as long as he doesn't take Job's life. It's all about Him. Job knew that. He said, "the Lord gave and the Lord has taken away; may the name of the Lord be praised" (Job 1:21) and "shall we accept good from God, and not trouble?" (Job 2:10).

One of the first things that I learned from the missionary who helped me learn how to study the Bible was something that has helped me so much. She said, "The Bible is about one person—and He is God. And it's about the people who interacted with God." As I am going through this last cancer journey I'm straining to keep my eyes on Him. When the pain is at its worst I try to keep my eyes on Him. God is at work. He is speaking. And just like he did for Job, He has already set the boundaries for my suffering. I cannot see where they end, but He knows.

In 1659, a Puritan writer declared, "God, who is infinite and matchless in goodness, hath ordered our troubles, yea, many troubles to come trooping in upon us on every side. As our mercies, so our crosses seldom come single; they usually come treading one upon the heels of another; they are like April showers, no sooner is one over, but another comes. It's mercy that every affliction is not an execution, every correction not a damnation. The more the afflictions, the more the heart is raised heavenward."[4]

It can seem like that. Just as soon as you get out of one storm, another one comes up. Paul David Tripp says, "Moments of suffering are always transformational in some way. No one ever comes out of the unexpected, the unwanted, the difficult, and the discouraging unchanged. You will not rise out of tragedy the way you were before it overtook you."[5] The hard waves of suffering are how our God changes us for His purposes. It's how He chisels away at what does not look like Him and shapes us by His transforming grace.

How are you suffering right now? Are you able to move your heart heavenward? Are you able to keep your eyes fixed on Him? When pain is overwhelming it can be hard to pull your attention away from the pain and look to Him. It's hard. When my son Spencer died, it was like that for me.

UNTHINKABLE PAIN

Spencer died suddenly of a massive heart attack at the age of forty-four in January 1998. I followed the ambulance in my car and rushed into the emergency room. They wouldn't let me go in with him. They worked on him for about thirty minutes and the doctor came out and said, "We can't bring him back; but we're going to try again." Another five or six minutes later he came back and brought me into the room. I walked around the hospital bed and touched his face. He was gone. It was the most traumatic experience of my life. I felt like a part of me had died. There was a white chaplain in the room with us. He came over and put his arms around my shoulder. I felt like I would have died if he hadn't put his arm around me. Every time I see him we talk about this. Parents are not supposed to bury their children. Children are supposed to bury their parents.

I spoke out of my grief at his funeral service. "God, I'm really mad at You. You took my son." My pain and my grief were too burdensome to take anywhere but to the throne room of heaven. Like Job, I understood that the Lord had given, and the Lord had taken away. Because God is sovereign, He can do that.

We read the story of Job and we have the benefit of knowing how God was involved from the very beginning. But Job didn't know any of that. He had no idea that God was about to commend him to Satan—for suffering and testing. He was minding his own business, and suddenly everything about his life changed.

And what Job did and said right after that is so very powerful: he worshiped the Lord, and he blessed His name. He worshiped and he blessed the Lord. He couldn't have done that if his eyes weren't fixed on the Lord. I'm not talking about ignoring pain or pretending that it's not there. I've heard so many people talk about not claiming that when it comes to pain and suffering. I'm talking about looking right through your pain into His strength. That's where joy lives in the midst of suffering. It's in Him. It's in that place where suffering wrestles you to the ground and you flail around in anger and desperation. You finally wear yourself out and surrender the fight. It's then that you realize His presence ... that He is with you. In your deepest, darkest pain He is with you. You find yourself leaning into Him for strength, and the power to put one foot in front of the other for one more day. He gives you strength through His Word to stand tall. The old preacher used to say, "He will prop you up on every leaning side."

When I struggled with the loss of Spencer I wasn't nearly as noble as Job. My first thought wasn't to worship God. I wanted to bargain with Him. I told Him I was angry because He took Spencer from me. I said that I would have given him to God, but He didn't give me a chance. I don't think I would have ever willingly given my son up, but I asked the Lord to give him back to me and allow me to return him. I later repented of my anger and prayed, "Lord, would You make him a fruit bearer for reconciliation?" That had been his life's work and I wanted his death to mean something. I had been involved in the movement just on the fringes and didn't know then that my commitment to the cause of reconciliation would be the fruit from his death. Over the weeks and months after he passed, doors began to be opened for me to speak on reconciliation. I would have much rather had Spencer, but I was motivated to work for the cause that he was so passionate about, as a way to keep his memory alive. God allowed me to pick up the mantle and run to people and places that I never dreamed of. He taught me how to press into Him for purpose and for joy. And I rejoice to think that I am still running ... though slower ... still running until my day is done.

There were many times after his death that someone who had not lost a child would try to comfort me by saying, "You'll be okay, John. You'll get over it." I don't think that's true. I don't think you ever get over losing a child. This is a hurt that is still fresh in my heart today. It has not healed. It still brings tears to my eyes whenever I talk about him. It has given me a zeal for other parents who lose a child. I want them to know that I understand what they're going through. I want to weep with them and bring them comfort in their loss.

Job knew the truth of God's sovereignty. God is in charge. Satan is not in charge. Sickness is not in charge. Calamity is not in charge. God is in charge. God chooses to wound us. God chooses to bruise us. God chooses.

> The hammer is a useful tool, but the nail, if it had feelings and intelligence, could present another side of the story. For the nail knows the hammer only as an opponent, a brutal, merciless enemy who lives to pound it into submission, to beat it down out of sight and clinch it into place. That is the nail's view of the hammer, and it is accurate, except for one thing: The nail forgets that both it and the hammer are servants of the same workman. Let the nail but remember that the hammer is held by the workman and all resentment toward it will disappear. The carpenter decides whose head will be beaten next and what hammer shall be used in the beating. That is his sovereign right. When the nail has surrendered to the will of the workman and has gotten a little glimpse of his benign plans for its future it will yield to the hammer without complaint.[6]

God is sovereign. He does choose. But I also have to remember again and again the lessons from the garden. The God who allows me to suffer is the God who loves me. He loves me. He loves me. That was settled on the cross at Calvary. He proved His love for me. Oh, how He loves you and me!

But, if I'm honest, every once in a while I still struggle with the lingering question of the "why" of it all . . .

CHAPTER TWO

The Unanswerable "Why"

"Why was I not hidden away in the ground like a stillborn child,
like an infant who never saw the light of day?"

JOB 3:16

B y this time, not only has Job lost all his earthly possessions and all his children, his body has suffered the enemy's attack and is falling apart. In his anguish he curses
the day he was born and asks the question so many of us wrestle
with when we suffer: *Why?*

"**Why** have you made me your target? Have I become a burden to
you? **Why** do you not pardon my offenses and forgive my sins?"
(Job 7:20b–21a)

"**Why** then did you bring me out of the womb? I wish I had died
before any eye saw me." (Job 10:18)

It's not hard to understand why Job was so troubled in his
spirit. He didn't know what we know about his suffering. And his

suffering had taken in everything that was his. The image had to be hard to look at: Job with open sores all over his body, sitting out on a dust heap, scratching and in agony. It was like that for his friends who came to comfort him. It was hard for them to look at what he had become: "When they saw him from a distance, they could hardly recognize him; they began to weep aloud, and they tore their robes and sprinkled dust on their heads" (Job 2:12).

THE STING OF POVERTY

Some suffering is so ugly and so heinous that it's hard to even talk about. You don't want to think that life can be that hard and that difficult for anybody. The pictures of starving children whose bellies are bloated because they have no food or water are hard to look at. When cancer or some other terminal disease begins to destroy the body, it can be hard to look at. When violence takes a life before its time, that's hard to think about.

When I think about what it was like for my mother to literally die of starvation in a land of plenty, I want to know how that could have happened. My family were sharecroppers in rural Mississippi during the Great Depression. Malnutrition was commonplace because cotton replaced food crops, and over time the soil became degraded. There just wasn't enough food for poor folks to survive. When you've been poor, you know that poverty isn't just about not having things. It's also about what it does to your soul to know that you are seen as less than others. It can be a deep, deep hurt.

She held on to life as long as she could, but she died when I was only seven months old. And I would have likely died too if it hadn't been for a lady who had a milk cow and knew that my mother had died. She made sure I had milk every day and was able to survive. That milk was a lifeline for me.

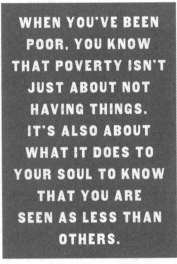

WHEN YOU'VE BEEN POOR, YOU KNOW THAT POVERTY ISN'T JUST ABOUT NOT HAVING THINGS. IT'S ALSO ABOUT WHAT IT DOES TO YOUR SOUL TO KNOW THAT YOU ARE SEEN AS LESS THAN OTHERS.

I think about that now when I see so many people standing in lines for food. We are in the middle of what the experts call a hunger emergency that is more severe than we've ever seen before. They expected the number of people facing acute hunger to reach 265 million by the end of 2020.[1] Back in 1968 I was blessed to speak before Senator George McGovern's Select Committee on Nutrition and Human Needs. I was able to talk about my mother dying from starvation and how important it is for poor folks to have healthy diets. That "committee developed a bipartisan response to hunger and laid the foundation of our current food assistance programs."[2] And a few years later Rev. Art Simon worked with a group of religious leaders to form Bread for the World. I was privileged to serve on that board. And I rejoice to see that this organization is still working to end hunger under the leadership of Eugene Cho. But it grieves my heart that there is still such a dire need today in such a rich country. Why so much suffering? Why does God allow so much suffering? Why did God take everything from Job, even all of his children? Why? Why?

THE POWER OF LAMENT

Maybe that's your question too. "Why, God? Why did this terrible thing happen to me?" That *why* comes from the depths of the soul and is a lament. I'm grateful that God allows us to ask why. We don't have to pray pretty prayers when we are suffering. We don't have to cross all the "t's" and dot all the "i's" when we are in agony. We don't have to pray theologically correct prayers when we are hurting. We can just cry out! Pain and agony ask the question, "Why? Why am I suffering like this?"

When I'm in deep pain I cry out, "God, have mercy on me!" And He hears my feeble cry. That's really what lament is. It's crying out to God, and there's something about a child of God crying out to his heavenly Father that gets His attention.

In *Weep with Me*, Mark Vroegop defines lament as "a prayer in pain that leads to trust. . . . Lament is the historic biblical prayer language of Christians in pain. It's the voice of God's people while living in a broken world."[3]

More than one-third of the psalms are devoted to lament. And the book of Lamentations is full of Jeremiah pouring out his heart to God in lament. I remember Spencer saying, "You play 'Amazing Grace' on the black keys, and you play it to the tune of the sound of the groan of the dying slaves." I think that's what they call the minor keys. They tug at your soul. Lament

> I REMEMBER SPENCER SAYING, "YOU PLAY 'AMAZING GRACE' ON THE BLACK KEYS, AND YOU PLAY IT TO THE TUNE OF THE SOUND OF THE GROAN OF THE DYING SLAVES."

tugs at your soul. It goes deep into the reservoir of pain.

When the psalm writers would pour out their lament they began with their complaint. They did what Job did. They cried out to God, they made their requests of Him . . . but they always ended with praise or a word of trust. Job did that in his lament:

> "I know that my redeemer lives,
>   and that in the end he will stand on the earth.
> And after my skin has been destroyed,
>   yet in my flesh I will see God;
> I myself will see him
>   with my own eyes—I, and not another."
> (Job 19:25–27)

I think maybe the church has got it wrong. We need to make room for lament. We need to let people know that God allows us to lament. We don't have to act like we're strong when we're falling apart. In Gary Smalley and John Trent's *The Blessing*, they have an entire chapter devoted to the idea that the church needs to be a place where we can take our hurts. They begin the chapter with a poem titled, "If This Is Not the Place." It asks the question, if the church is not the place where we can go to cry when we hurt, then where can we go? And it challenges the notion that you have to always be smiling and have your happy face on. Life is hard. And it becomes harder when we don't have safe places to share our grief and our struggles without being made to feel like we're not strong enough. We need a place where we can hurt together, cry together, heal together. I think that place should be the church.

In *This Too Shall Last: Finding Grace When Suffering Lingers*, K. J. Ramsey says, "The tacit message in our churches, culture, and relationships is this: success is public; suffering is private. We see so little of each other's insides that we come to believe we might be the only ones suffering. We hide our wounds behind bandages of our own making while wondering if the hard things lingering in our lives somehow delineate between who belongs to God's family and who doesn't. Hiding and hurting, we become divorced from hope and detached from joy."[3] We've got to find a way to give space to our cries and our hurts when we come together as the body of Christ.

HE ANSWERS WITH HIMSELF

It reveals a lot about God that He allowed Job thirty-four of the forty-two chapters to lament and wrestle with God and his friends before He finally spoke into the conversation. God makes room for our lament, for our questions, for our heartache. I love that He came to Job. He let him hang out there for a while, but He finally came. And He actually engaged in a dialogue with Job! The Creator of the universe gave Job the privilege of having a one-on-one conversation with Him. He came to Job. And to his question of why . . . God filled that space with Himself. He didn't explain anything to Job about His conversation with Satan and His offering Job as a worthy target. Nothing. Silence. And for much of life it's like that. There is no answer that will suffice for why a child is born with a deformity. There is no answer that will do for why a family is murdered by an intruder. No answer that will suffice for why cancer comes back again, destroying what was left from before. There is only the answer that He provided to Job: "Here I AM." And what we, like Job, are left with is the question that Helen Roseveare wrestled with:

Helen Roseveare, a British medical missionary in the Congo uprising when the Mau-Mau revolutionaries invaded, was attacked. This godly, gracious, woman of God was raped, assaulted, humiliated, hanging on with her life to a faith that would not be shaken. While recovering from that horrible event, Helen and the Lord grew closer together than they had ever been before. In her pain, she felt his presence and sensed him asking her: "Can you thank Me for trusting you with this experience, even if I never tell you why?"[4]

At first, she wasn't sure that she could ever thank Him for her experience, but one word was riveted in her heart: *privilege*. She had been given the privilege of suffering. God had entrusted her with a special, and very difficult—almost unthinkable—type of suffering. Like Job, she was given the privilege of suffering. I have been given the privilege of suffering. If you're reading this book you probably have been given that privilege too.

That's a paradox, isn't it? That anyone would consider suffering a *privilege*. We'll talk about that more in the coming chapters. But for now, let's rivet our hearts to the truth that God doesn't always answer the why in our hearts. And that's probably for the best. I'm not sure any answer would ease the pain of the death of a loved spouse or betrayal by a close, intimate friend. No answer would make the suffering of infertility or moral failure any less.

In that huge space of unanswered questions for Helen Roseveare, for Job, for me, and for you, God offers Himself. He is there. He is present. The God who knows about suffering is there. The God who loves me—He is there. He is there with awesome power to keep me. He is there. The old preacher used to say, "He's my everything. He's water in dry places. He's bread in a starving land. He's a doctor in a sickroom, a lawyer in a courtroom. He's my everything." He's there filling the void when I don't understand why. He is enough. He's more than enough . . . and that's joy!

CHAPTER THREE

Tested by Suffering

"Skin for skin!" Satan replied. "A man will give all he has for his own life.
But now stretch out your hand and strike his flesh and bones,
and he will surely curse you to your face."

JOB 2:4–5

S atan was convinced that Job only loved, worshiped, and
served the Lord because He blessed him with good things.
He argued that all Job wanted from God was His goodness and His blessings. He refused to accept the possibility that
even if God allowed him to strip Job of every possession he
owned, and then touch his body, he still would not curse God.
Satan's argument was that Job would do whatever it took to save
his own life and end his suffering—even if it meant cursing God.

Suffering tests our faith, and I think that suffering asks each
of us the same questions: *Will I remain faithful to Him through
this? Am I drawing closer to Him or pulling further away during
this time of difficulty? Is my love for Him growing stronger, or am I
finding myself angry and resentful toward Him?* Those can be hard
questions to answer while you're going through hard trials. But
they stare us in the face and won't allow us to avoid them.

I don't know what you're going through right now, but I do

know that if you are suffering, you are being tempted to draw away from Him. While God is testing and drawing us, the enemy is tempting and wooing us. And his temptations always are meant to lead us to sin in one of three ways: 1) the lust of the flesh; 2) the lust of the eyes; or 3) the pride of life. He tried all these temptations on Jesus when He was at the end of His forty-day fast in the wilderness. When He was hungry, exhausted, and weary, Satan mounted his attack. And he does the same for us. When our suffering is at its worst he offers us an escape that always is meant to dull the pain and draw us away from God.

THE LUST OF THE FLESH

The lust of the flesh is doing what pleases the flesh, and Satan is always tempting us to do this. He tempted Jesus by suggesting that He should turn stones into bread because He was hungry. He was right. Jesus was hungry. But turning stones into bread was not how God intended for Him to be fed. He had to trust His Father's plan. And the enemy tempted Job, through his wife, to put an end to his suffering by cursing God and dying. Job's suffering had to be unbelievable. The agony must have been so deep. But ending it all is never God's way.

After my surgery the pain was so intense. I was desperate for some kind of relief. And I was so thankful that the doctors had hooked me up to a morphine drip. I could pump the button when I needed it. And the temptation is to never stop pushing that button.

When our suffering is at its worst the temptation is to do anything to stop the pain. This is sometimes where Satan does his greatest work. He steps in with an alternative to the pain. The morphine drip was a wonderful thing. But at some point, I had to wean myself off it. At some point I had to accept that a certain level of pain was going to be necessary if I was ever going to heal and be free from the need for morphine.

> **WHEN OUR SUFFERING IS AT ITS WORST THE TEMPTATION IS TO DO ANYTHING TO STOP THE PAIN.**

My friend Andraé Crouch suffered and struggled so much in this area and a lot of his songs came out of that struggle. The words to "Through It All" remind us of what we need to do when we are tested beyond our limits:

Through it all
I've learned to trust in Jesus . . .
I've learned to depend upon His Word
I thank God for the mountains
And I thank Him for the valleys
I thank Him for the storms He brought me through.[1]

LUST OF THE EYES

In *The Bondage Breaker*, Neil Anderson defines the lust of the eyes in this way: "We see what the world has to offer and desire it above our relationship with God. . . . Fueled by the lust for what we see, we grab for all we can get, believing that we need it and trying to justify the idea that God wants us to have it."[2] When we are suffering, the lure of the world is great. It offers relief and escape from the pain. It offers us diversions that numb our pain.

Psalm 73:2–3 reminds us of how important our perspective is while we are going through the valley of suffering. "But as for me, my feet had almost slipped; I had nearly lost my foothold. For I envied the arrogant when I saw the prosperity of the wicked." We can become embittered when we see others prospering and doing well while we are struggling to serve the Lord and receive suffering and calamity as a reward. We can get into the comparison game, almost feeling like we are getting the short end of the stick and that God should do better by us because we belong to Him. Thanks be to God that the same psalm helps us see the remedy for this kind of thinking. The psalmist remembered the end of all things—that the day will come when God will right the scales. That remembrance caused him to declare, "Those who are far from you will perish; you destroy all who are unfaithful to you. But as for me, it is good to be near God. I have made the Sovereign Lord my refuge; I will tell of all your deeds" (Ps. 73:27–28).

I've had to work hard to keep my eyes on Him while I'm going through hard times. Not looking to the left or to the right at how others are doing. Those distractions can turn you away from suffering well.

THE PRIDE OF LIFE

I think we all know what pride is. It's thinking more of ourselves than we should. It's putting ourselves in the place of God in our own lives. Doing what we want to do, instead of considering and obeying His will. Suffering exposes this in our hearts. It did that for Job. He protested against his three friends and declared that he had not done anything to defraud the poor or to mistreat anyone. He was probably right. He had not done any of the big sins that his friends accused him of doing. They stopped talking to him "because he was righteous in his own eyes" (Job 32:1). But his fourth friend, Elihu, hit on something. And as soon as he finished talking to Job, God showed up. Elihu accused Job of being prideful: "Do you think this is just? You say, 'I am in the right, not God'" (Job 35:2).

It was right after that when God spoke up. And He corrected Job and his three older friends, but He did not challenge anything that Elihu had said. Job had to be humbled. Satan thought that Job would curse God. He didn't win that wager—but it was true that Job needed to be humbled. Suffering has a way of attacking our pride. Job was rich and respected by everyone. But when God struck him, he lost all those things that he had prided himself on in life.

Anthony Evans, the son of Tony Evans, spoke at his mother's homegoing recently. He talked about coming to terms with this truth, as the Lord chose not to heal his mother of terminal cancer. He confessed to having an entitlement mentality. He had felt like God owed it to their family because they had been so faithful to Him. Their family is known for powerful Bible preaching and teaching around the world. But God let him know that He didn't need anyone's suggestions on how He can get the glory out of a situation. I think a lot of us good Christians feel this way. We can have an entitlement mentality that suggests that God shouldn't let us suffer—because we're the good ones. But God doesn't owe us anything. We owe Him everything.

A lot of people tell me that they're amazed that I'm so humble. They'll never know how

> **WE CAN HAVE AN ENTITLEMENT MENTALITY THAT SUGGESTS THAT GOD SHOULDN'T LET US SUFFER— BECAUSE WE'RE THE GOOD ONES.**

much pride I struggle with. Like Anthony Evans, I have struggled with entitlement. It's been a constant struggle for me to not think too highly of myself. We can think that we're pretty mature in our faith—after all, we know the Scriptures. We have walked with the Lord for a long time. But when the right kind of suffering hits, we really discover what we're made of.

If we are children of God, I really believe that we don't faint—the virtues of the fruit of the spirit will keep us from fainting. We may stumble but we don't fall. In spite of it all, Job held on. He persevered in his complaint, repeatedly calling out to God for answers. I think he teaches us to keep going back to God and asking our questions. It's human and natural to have questions. God is big enough to handle every question of our hearts. He's big enough to handle our disappointments and even our anger.

BEARING FRUIT

When it's all said and done . . . we stand. Through pain and through agony. Through loss and through failure. Through every kind of suffering. The Holy Spirit within us holds us up, as He develops the fruit of patience and gentleness. This fruit, above all, matters when we go through suffering.

Patience

The old preachers used to say, "You can't hurry God." And I believe that. When we're going through the test of suffering, the most important thing to us is getting past it. We want it to be done. We want to know how long we have to endure the pain. I'm learning the truth of what Isaiah said: "But those who hope in the LORD will renew their strength. They will soar on wings like eagles; they will run and not grow weary, they will walk and not be faint" (Isa. 40:31). I'm waiting on Him and finding that He is giving me just enough strength to make it one more day.

When the Bible talks about patience (*hupomeno*) it means "under misfortunes and trials to hold fast to one's faith in Christ."[3] When we suffer, the temptation is great to turn away from the things of Christ. But we have the story of Job that encourages us to hold on until the end. We don't know what God has in store for us, just on the other side of our suffering.

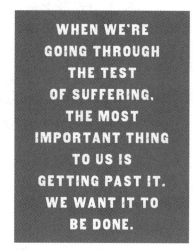

WHEN WE'RE GOING THROUGH THE TEST OF SUFFERING, THE MOST IMPORTANT THING TO US IS GETTING PAST IT. WE WANT IT TO BE DONE.

"As you know, we count as blessed those who have persevered. You have heard of Job's perseverance and have seen what the Lord finally brought about. The Lord is full of compassion and mercy" (James 5:11).

I think of the suffering of Joseph and how he had to patiently endure mistreatment from his brothers. Then he had to endure the false accusation of Potiphar's wife and unfair imprisonment. And after all of that, just when he probably thought he was going to get out of prison, the chief cupbearer broke his promise and Joseph ended up in prison for two more years. And God elevated him to a place of power because of his obedience. When he had the opportunity to take revenge on his brothers because of what they had done to him, he showed meekness and kindness. He told them to come close. That's a word of compassion. He said, "I forgive you. You meant it for evil, but God meant it for good."

Patient endurance had produced a heart of kindness. He welcomed them and took care of them during the years of famine. That's the kind of patience the Lord is looking for from us when we are going through our trials.

Gentleness

Gentleness (*prautes*) means to be mild-spirited and meek. When we're suffering it can be easy to strike out at others because of our own pain. It can be tempting to give ourselves a pass on being kind and considerate of others because of our own suffering. But the power of the Holy Spirit within us can give us the grace to be kind and tender with those who are around us. That's especially important for family members who may carry the heavy load of taking care of us. I've had to think about this a lot as I have suffered with my cancer over the last year. When I am in pain I need to remember to be gracious and kind. Pain can make you irritable and impatient with the very people who are taking care of you.

One of the most powerful pictures of gentleness is what Jesus did while He hung on a cross in excruciating pain. His enemies stood before him, taunting Him and gambling for His clothes. He spoke no harsh words against them. Instead He said, "Father, forgive them, for they do not know what they are doing" (Luke 23:34). He could have called down legions of angels to defend Himself, but He submitted to their torture and prayed for them.

SUFFERING TESTS FAMILY

Suffering doesn't just test the sufferer. It tests the entire family. When we suffer, our family suffers with us. Every parent whose child is suffering suffers right along with that child. Every one of those parents would eagerly take their child's suffering and put it on themselves if they could. To have to watch your child suffer is torment.

Many times, marriages fall apart because of intense suffering. It's easier to blame the other person and walk away than to stay together and work through the pain. Job's wife's words reveal a lot: "Are you still maintaining your integrity? Curse God and die!" (Job 2:9). Her words are an indication of the stress that Job's suffering had put on their marriage. She also had lost all her children—all ten of them—and

TO HAVE TO WATCH YOUR CHILD SUFFER IS TORMENT.

all her worldly possessions. She was angry. She was bitter. Husbands and wives have to make the hard decision that they will weather the storms of life together, "in sickness and in health . . . for richer, for poorer."

I've been so blessed to have had a wonderful wife by my side through one storm after another. The first storm almost destroyed us. I've not talked a lot about it, but early in our marriage after I came back from the Korean war I was not true to my vows. Vera Mae left me and went back to her family. She was pregnant with Spencer at the time. She came back to me when Spencer was six months old. When I first laid eyes on my son my love for her grew so deep. She forgave me, and we worked hard to restore trust in our marriage. Since that time, she has never wavered in her love and her devotion for these seventy years. And now, as we near the end of life, it's my turn to care for her. It is a labor of love to make sure all her needs are met. And somehow in our caring for one another in our difficult moments our love has grown deeper still.

As I am closing in on the final chapter of my life, I see things clearer than I did before. One of the hardest things about getting to this point in life is looking back and experiencing regret. Wishing you had done things differently. That's its own kind of deep pain because you can't change what is past. You can only learn from it and move forward. I wish I had been more present as a father. I wish I had expressed more love to my daughters when they were growing up. They've said that because I didn't grow up in an intact family I never learned how to give them the love they needed. That's their experience, and it's painful in how it affects our relationship today. I believe that I worked hard to provide for them, to give them the things they needed. Maybe I gave too much of the things, and not enough of myself.

> **ONE OF THE HARDEST THINGS ABOUT GETTING TO THIS POINT IN LIFE IS LOOKING BACK AND EXPERIENCING REGRET.**

Family pain can be a deep, deep pain. When David wrote Psalm 3 I think this may have been the lowest point in his life, other than the incident with Bathsheba. I think these psalms were written so they would never be forgotten. They remind us that life is hard. And when we are in the hard places we can call out to our Lord. David is fleeing from his own son, Absalom. He had a mixed-up love for this son. He had spoiled Absalom and overlooked the things he was doing. Absalom had killed his own half-brother to avenge the rape of his sister, Tamar. He was a good-looking guy and used his deceitfulness at the city gate to win the hearts of the people. Now David's family had been wrecked, and his own son was coming to kill him. In his pain he wrote, "LORD, how many are my foes! How many rise up against me! Many are saying of me, 'God will not deliver him'" (Ps. 3:1–2).

It's hard when the person who is causing you to suffer is someone in your own family. Families suffer when they don't deal with issues and heal from them. Parents hurt children and children hurt parents. Each new day offers the opportunity and time to heal the hurts that linger. David found healing as he looked to the Lord: "But you, LORD, are a shield around me, my glory, the One who lifts my head high" (Ps. 3:3).

SUFFERING TESTS FRIENDS

Suffering tests friends as well. It shows us who our true friends are. It's been said that it's okay to get sick; but don't stay sick too long because people will fade away. It's just human nature to want to see an end to things. We want to set limits—not just on other people's suffering, but also on how long we will hang in there. Job's friends' patience ran out after they realized that he wasn't going to admit to any big sin that would explain his suffering. They figured that they would help him identify what sin he had committed that caused his great downfall. And then they expected him to repent and God to forgive him. But it didn't work out like that.

When we are suffering, many friends may come alongside

us—in the beginning. But some of those friendships may not last through the long haul. I've been trying to be the kind of friend who hangs in there with my friends when they are going through the valley of suffering. God has blessed me with some of those kinds of friends and it has meant the world to me. It seems like they have pulled even closer as we have struggled to continue to care for Vera Mae at home.

> MY FRIENDS HAVE COME ALONGSIDE US AND SHOWN THEMSELVES TO BE FAITHFUL, FAITHFUL FRIENDS. THIS HAS BEEN SO PRECIOUS TO ME.

I talked earlier about psychological pain. It's fearing what you don't know. I've been tormented with fear about whether we have enough resources to carry us into the future if the Lord allows us to remain. My friends have come alongside us and shown themselves to be faithful, faithful friends. This has been so precious to me.

ARE YOU PASSING THE TEST?

James Hewitt said, "Life is a grindstone. Whether it grinds you down or polishes you up depends upon what you are made of."[4] I do believe that suffering is a test. God uses it to grow me up in my faith, to help me trust Him more. Sometimes He uses it to discipline my behavior, to correct me when I move outside of His will. And every test is an opportunity for the enemy to tempt me to seek relief through the lust of the flesh, the lust of the eyes, or the pride of life. Job was clear that he had not mistreated the poor or done any of the things that his friends accused him of doing. But when confronted by Elihu and then the Lord, he had to admit that pride had gotten the best of him. His suffering helped him to see himself differently: "I despise myself and repent in dust and ashes" (Job 42:6).

I think that pain and suffering get under us in a way that causes us to confess. It humbles us. It breaks us. And maybe that's the secret. That's how we pass the test. It's through brokenness. "Brokenness is the shattering of my self-will—the absolute surrender of my will to the will of God. Brokenness is the stripping of self-reliance and independence from God."[5] I become broken when I realize that no amount of money or influence or status can fix my situation. I cry out to Him because I realize that He is the only one who can change my circumstances, heal my hurts, fix my dilemma. I pass the test when I realize my desperate need for Him. Oh, how I need Him! The songwriter Annie Sherwood Hawks said it best when she wrote, "I need Thee, Oh, I Need thee. Ev'ry hour I need Thee. Oh, bless me now, my Savior. I come to Thee!"

CHAPTER FOUR

I See Him

"My ears had heard of you but now my eyes have seen you.
Therefore I despise myself and repent in dust and ashes."

JOB 42:5–6

Everything that Job had and depended on was gone: his children, his wealth, his health. All he was left with was God . . . and He had been silent. Job was in the middle of some hard testing ground. But now God has finally spoken into the silence and challenged Job's knowledge of Him. "Then the Lord spoke to Job out of the storm. He said: 'Who is this that obscures my plans with words without knowledge?'" (Job 38:1–2). "Will the one who contends with the Almighty correct him? Let him who accuses God answer him!" (Job 40:2)

I believe that when God tests us through suffering He's looking to see what we really know about Him. *Is my theology right? Do I really know God, or do I just know about God?* Suffering helped Job see God rightly. He had to acknowledge that God is awesome. God is good. God is sovereign . . . and so much more.

GOD IS WITH YOU IN THE DARKNESS

In her book *Breathe*, my friend Kay Warren talks about her desperation to find God when her son, Matthew, attempted suicide for the first time.[1] Because her overwhelming feeling was "darkness," she studied the Scriptures looking for what God says about it. She came across Isaiah 45:3, where God promises to use King Cyrus to free His people from Babylon: "I will give you the treasures of darkness and riches hidden in secret places so that you may know that it is I, the Lord God of Israel, who calls you by your name" (NRSV). Kay had to decide whether she trusted and believed that God could bring "treasure" out of the darkness and despair in her heart. She chose to believe Him, and He was faithful—both after her son's suicide attempt and again years later, when Matthew did take his own life.

At two points in my life I have been at that place where death seemed like the answer. I was in so much emotional torment and pain that it seemed the only way out. They say there are five stages of grief, and I'm pretty sure I had gone through anger, denial, and bargaining with the Lord. But I was stuck in depression. One of those times was when I was losing control of the Voice of Calvary ministry and felt like I had lost any reason to carry on. In my frustration and anger over losing the ministry, I had said things that hurt a lot of people. Pain can carry you to the point of death—and you begin to weigh whether that's what you really want. Or not.

In a moment of deep despair, I called my friend H. Spees and said, "I don't know if I'm gonna make it." He jumped in his car and found me on the floor, sobbing and shaking. He stayed with me through the night, letting me unburden my heart. He helped me see God in all of that darkness. That gave me a glimmer of hope. God Himself was the treasure in that darkness and He gave me the courage to keep moving forward.

Some people turn to liquor when the pain gets that hard. Others turn to drugs. I don't really believe that people actually want to die when they overdose. I think they just want the pain and suffering to go away. I think that's the idea of the song, "One Day at a Time." If we can just hold on for one more day, we can trust that the same God who brought us this far will keep us.

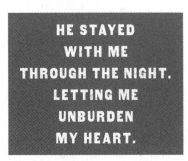

HE STAYED WITH ME THROUGH THE NIGHT, LETTING ME UNBURDEN MY HEART.

Maybe you're at that point now. Feeling like it's all over. Like there's no reason to keep pushing on through pain that gets worse rather than better day by day. You can take all that pain to Him. He is waiting for you. He hears your faintest cry. He will hold you. He will keep you. I beg you to trust Him.

GOD IS GOOD

"God is good all the time; All the time, God is good." You can begin that saying with another believer and they will finish it for you. It has become a part of our culture to answer this refrain enthusiastically. It seems like this is the first thing that we say when we are blessed with what we want. When we get a new car, a new house, or a job promotion, we eagerly say, "God is good!" But what do we say in our hearts when we experience a significant loss, when we lose our job, or our home burns to the ground, or our adoption process falls through? Can we still declare that God is good?

God's goodness has to do with His character. *He* is good. When life is hard we need to cling to the truths from Scripture that remind us of His goodness:

> "Taste and see that the LORD is good; blessed is the one who takes refuge in him." (Ps. 34:8)

> "Give thanks to the LORD, for he is good; his love endures forever." (Ps. 107:1)

> "The LORD is good to all; he has compassion on all he has made." (Ps. 145:9)

Author and pastor Ray Pritchard tells the story of the night his son was in a terrible car accident with some of his friends. They hit a tree at a high rate of speed, but by God's grace, no one was killed. The engineer who visited the scene of the accident the next day said that if the car had hit the tree at a slightly different angle all the boys would have been dead. At a worship service the following week many of the members said, "Isn't God good? He spared the boys' lives!"

Ray's wife, Marlene, responded, "Many of you know that our oldest son and his friends barely survived a terrible wreck. And some people have told us that God was good to spare Joshua and the others who were with him. It's true that God was good to us, but God would have been good even if Joshua had died in the wreck."[2]

In the midst of our suffering I think Satan asks us, "Is God still good?" He whispers in our hearts, "If God was really good, He wouldn't allow you to hurt like this . . . If He was a good God, He wouldn't have allowed your marriage to fall apart. He wouldn't have allowed your house to be broken into. He wouldn't have afflicted you with cancer."Those are all the devil's lies. A good God does allow all those things to happen. And none of those things take away from His goodness. He assures us that all those things will work together for the good for those of us who are the called according to His purposes. He will work it all out for good. We don't know how . . . but we know God is good, and that is what matters.

I can't allow my suffering to make me think bad about God. I can't allow my pain to make me challenge the character of God. He is good even when my circumstances are bad. He is faithful— even when everybody and everything else fails. He is worthy of all praise and glory even when my life is turned upside down. The songwriter had it right, "You can't make me doubt Him. I know too much about Him."

GOD IS SOVEREIGN

Suffering tests whether I really understand what the sovereignty of God means. I think in its simplest terms it means that God can do whatever He wants to do, whenever and however He chooses. He doesn't have to answer to anyone else. He doesn't need my permission to test me. I think this truth about God really goes against our Western way of thinking. We think we should chart our own path. We don't like the idea that someone else makes the decisions about what will and what won't happen in our lives.

Job acknowledged early on that it is the Lord who gives and takes away. The sovereignty of God forces us to recognize that all we have is from Him. None of us decided which family we were going to be born into. We didn't choose our parents or our

GOD DOESN'T NEED MY PERMISSION TO TEST ME.

siblings. And we don't choose what kind of suffering we will endure. That's God's choice. He knows what hammer to use to chisel the rough places in my heart. He knows what storm will break my heart and make it earnestly seek Him.

When Job finally had his face-to-face encounter with God, he said, "I know that you can do all things; no purpose of yours can be thwarted" (Job 42:2). He understood fully what it means for God to be in charge of your life. He charts our path. He hems us in. He marks out the boundaries for our territory.

It was trust in the sovereignty of God that kept my ancestors going through the pain, ugliness, and degradation of slavery. They had faith in God that helped them accept what they could not understand. They would say things like "His ways are as far above our ways as the east is from the west." And they sang songs like "We'll Understand It Better By and By" and "Swing Low, Sweet Chariot . . . coming for to carry me home." These songs were born out of a struggle that at its core believed in the sovereignty of an almighty God.

HE IS WITH ME

Suffering can cause us to feel like we are all by ourselves. Nobody knows the trouble we're going through. Nobody understands the depth of our misery. It's in these moments when the enemy whispers this lie to us, "God doesn't care about what you're going through. He's left you here all by yourself."

I'm grateful for the truth of the Word that assures us that

God is everywhere at the same time. In *Basic Theology*, Charles Ryrie explains the omnipresence of God in this way: "God is everywhere present with His whole being at all times."[3] He is with me in my moments of doubt. He is with me when my faith wavers. He is with me in my anger and in my frustration. When I am weary and want to quit . . . He is there.

The psalmist reminds us of that truth:

Where can I go from your Spirit?
> Where can I flee from your presence?
If I go up to the heavens, you are there;
> if I make my bed in the depths, you are there.
If I rise on the wings of the dawn,
> if I settle on the far side of the sea,
even there your hand will guide me,
> your right hand will hold me fast.
(Ps. 139:7–10)

Hagar discovered that truth in the wilderness. She had become pregnant by Abraham, and Sarah had run her off. The angel of the Lord went after her and instructed her to return to Sarah. He promised that God would take care of her. Hagar exclaimed, "'You are the God who sees me,' for she said, 'I have now seen the One who sees me'" (Gen. 16:13). She named her son Ishmael, meaning "God hears." Our pain and suffering may drive us into the wilderness, but we can be assured that there is no place we can find ourselves where God is not with us and where we are not under His watchful eye. He is the God who sees us! We need to develop an expression of longing. We might say, "I'm here. Make Yourself real to me. I don't feel You, God. I don't see You walking with me." But He's been there all the time.

I REPENT IN DUST AND ASHES . . .

When Job finally got his audience with God, he was humbled. He finally realized the sin of pride that covered him. He came face to face with his willingness to charge God with unfairness in allowing him to suffer. He repented.

I think suffering strips us of our defenses and our excuses. It forces us to see where we stand before a holy God. And it beckons us to repent of those things that stand between us. Suffering offers us a powerful encounter with God, just like it did for Job. The God in us is patient with us. The big deal of grace is that God has given us the solution to the sin problem—that's His forgiveness. Most of the time when I start talking about sin, people start talking about somebody else's sin. Dietrich Bonhoeffer said, "Many Christians are unthinkably horrified when a real sinner is suddenly discovered among the righteous. So, we remain alone with our sin, living in lies and hypocrisy. The fact is that we *are* sinners!"[4]

We need to be awakened to our own sin. Many of our great heroes discovered their own sin. John Newton penned the words to "Amazing Grace" when he was struck with his own sin problem and the need for a Savior. My friend Chuck Colson said he would have walked over his grandmother's grave to do anything that Nixon had told him to do. He was so very proud that he was the president's personal advisor. But he discovered how wretched he was when he got Jesus in his life. The apostle John says, "If we claim to be without sin, we deceive ourselves and the truth is not in us" (1 John 1:8). I've come to believe that the "unpardonable sin" is that sin that you love so much that you refuse to confess it to God. Pain is His way of getting that out of us. When sin can be so deeply embedded in us, He uses pain to root it out. That's

Him trying to speak to us and purify us, to extract from us those dark things in our lives. It's an attention getter, a teaching vehicle that we might grow in grace and knowledge of Him. This is continual through life. I'm daily laying my sins before Him and rejoicing with gratitude that His blood still has the power to cleanse and to wash all my sins away.

God finally got what He wanted to get out of Job, after all his suffering and trial. Job had talked and talked and justified and justified himself. And finally, he repented and became silent before the great I AM. In His tender mercy He received Job's confession, and then he told him to pray for his friends. I think God was still testing Job even at this point. I think Job finally passed the test. He still loved his buddies. When he prayed for them, the healing began. God blessed him with more than he had in the beginning. I'm sure that the joy Job experienced at this point was richer and deeper because of gratitude for God's mercy and grace.

HE IS ENOUGH

The place where you come to the end of yourself and there's just you and God—I call this the hiding place. It's where you're totally alone with God and you find the balm for your hurting soul. It's in Him. It's healing for your soul. For all your pain. All the distress. All the heartache. Lay it at His feet. He is the Rock of Ages. And we can hide ourselves in Him. It's a bit like this story:

> The *Seawanhaka* steamer burned at sea [in 1880]. One of the
> Fisk Jubilee singers was aboard. Before jumping into the sea
> he fastened life preservers on himself and his wife; but someone
> snatched hers away from her. In the water, however, she put

her hands on his shoulders and thus kept afloat until, almost exhausted, she said to her husband, "I cannot hold on any longer!" "Try a little longer," begged the agonized husband. "Let us sing 'Rock of Ages.'"

And as the hymn rang out over the waves, others almost sinking took up the strains of the pleading prayer to God. The hymn seemed to give new strength to many in that desperate hour. By and by a boat was seen approaching, and as it came nearer the singing was renewed until with superhuman efforts they laid hold upon the lifeboats and were carried to safety. The singer, in telling this story himself, declared that he believed this hymn had saved many lives, besides his own and his wife's, in that dreadful disaster.[5]

We believe in Jesus Christ, the Rock of Ages, and have all been saved from the sinking ship of sin. We have found Him to be an anchor and a rock. The old saints sang, "Jesus is a rock in a weary land. Shelter in the time of storm." I agree with Charles Spurgeon: "I have learned to kiss the wave that throws me against the Rock of Ages."[6]

We have weathered many storms. Seen much suffering. And I suppose that being chosen to suffer, through no fault of your own, is the hardest kind of suffering. It is hard. No smooth sounding words can change that. It is hard. But Job's story teaches us that He loves us enough to set the limits on our suffering, and in His tender mercy He draws us near. He comes close to help us carry the burden. I hope you feel His presence even now. He is with you. You are never alone. While He is working on us through suffering, He's preparing us to serve others who are hurting. Suffering prepares us to be His hands and feet to serve fellow sufferers. We'll go there in the next section . . .

PART TWO

WHEN
YOU CHOOSE
SUFFERING

CHAPTER FIVE

The Case for Suffering

"I have told you these things, so that in me you may have peace.
In this world you will have trouble. But take heart!
I have overcome the world."

JOHN 16:33

It's hard to make a case for suffering when the images of prosperity and success and wealth are flashed in front of us every time we turn on the television and even in some churches today. Jesus warned the multitude against the temptation to have more and more things: "Watch out! Be on your guard against all kinds of greed; life does not consist in an abundance of possessions" (Luke 12:15). And then He told the parable of the rich man who had so much that, instead of sharing it with others, he decided to build a bigger barn to store his stuff. "God said to him, 'You fool! This very night your life will be demanded from you. Then who will get what you have prepared for yourself?' This is how it will be with whoever stores up things for themselves but is not rich toward God" (Luke 12:20b–21).

Suffering is what we are called to in this life. Real joy comes when we are taking the pain of others, serving others, and always rejoicing in our gratitude for serving others. That's the joy right now. And this is the joy that causes us to keep bearing the pain. It's the gratitude of bearing that pain. We are more like Him when we are suffering. I believe that so deeply. We are most like our Lord when we choose to suffer.

My doctors said I should have died of a heart attack, but I think my heart has had to go through so much pain that the pain exercised my heart. And it is stronger because of the pain. I believe pain works something in you that strengthens you.

There is a land of no more suffering that we are all headed to if we belong to Him, but until we see heaven, we are called to suffer. I want to suggest that each of us is called to suffer in at least three different ways: 1) suffer for the advance of the gospel; 2) suffer for the cause of justice; and 3) suffer with fellow sufferers.

SUFFERING FOR THE ADVANCE OF THE GOSPEL

The early church made the right decision. They stood for what was right even when it cost them great suffering, even their lives. Ignatius of Antioch was condemned to die for his faith in Rome in AD 107. They had a lot of festivities planned to celebrate a military victory, so they sent him to Rome so that his death could provide some good entertainment. On his way to Rome he wrote seven letters that teach us a lot about what it was like being a Christian in those early days. When he heard that the Christians in Rome were planning to resist and challenge his death, he urged them not to do that. He wrote, "I am the wheat of God, and am ground by the teeth of the wild beasts, that I may be found the pure bread of God. . . . when I suffer, I shall be the freedman of Jesus Christ, and shall rise again free in Him."[1] Tradition says that Ignatius was sent to Rome and cast to the wild beasts.

Just reading those words challenges me to look again at how my level of suffering measures up. I've been through a lot. But I still come up short. I think most of us do. I wonder what it takes to come to that level of commitment to suffer for the cause of Christ. I'm sure that Ignatius didn't just stumble into that mindset. He had to have been taught and conditioned and convinced beyond the shadow of a doubt that when the rubber met the road this was what he would do. He had to have already made up his mind that when the time came, he would meet it boldly. I believe each of us should wrestle with that thought now. If the time comes, am I ready to die for Him?

An old preacher told the story of a large church that was in the midst of a rousing worship experience. Two gunmen walked in and toward the front of the sanctuary. They pointed their guns and said, "Everyone who is a believer in Jesus Christ, stand up!" There was empty silence. They waited. And before long three bold souls stood up, and each one said, "I believe in Jesus Christ." The gunmen demanded that everyone else leave the sanctuary. After it was cleared out, leaving only three brave souls, they said, "Now we can have church!"

If we are to suffer for the advance of the gospel we must be clear-minded and devoted in our commitment to our Lord. I love this excerpt from "Praying on the Armor of God" by my spiritual son, Dr. David Anderson. It shows us how we should pray before we begin this serious work:

I pray on the Gospel Shoes of Peace. I choose to stand in the shoes of your good news and on the firm foundation of Jesus Christ, the solid rock. All other ground is sinking sand. I pray that I will not slip or fall but that my feet would be firmly fitted on your lordship, Jesus. I choose to stand on you so that the peace of God which transcends all understanding will guard my heart and mind in Christ Jesus, the Rock of Ages. I receive your peace now, Jesus, from the sole of my feet to the crown of my head.[2]

We'll need to be covered by His peace in order to suffer well.

Lott Carey

Lott Carey was born into slavery just four years after the signing of the Declaration of Independence. He was raised on a plantation with his parents and his grandmother. His father and grandmother were committed believers. His grandmother instilled in him a passion for taking the gospel to her people in Africa. She loved the Lord and would often tell Lott about how much their people had suffered just making the long, hard journey from Africa to this country. She would regularly tell Lott about the rich heritage of their people and how her heart yearned for those who did not know Christ. Mihala knew that she would never be able to return to Africa, but her hopes were in her grandson, Lott. She would tell Lott, "Son, you will grow strong. You will lead many, and perhaps it may be you who will travel over the big seas to carry the great secret to my people."[3]

Lott heard the gospel message from John 3 and committed his life to Christ. He quickly learned to read and write, passionately studying the Bible. He was licensed to preach and soon found himself pastoring the African Baptist Church in

Richmond. It was a thriving ministry with eight hundred members. But the call to share the gospel in Africa was strong in his heart. He left all of that behind to follow the call to missions.

On January 23, 1821 his ship set sail to the continent of Africa, landing in Sierra Leone. In his last sermon before his departure, Lott Carey left his congregation with this assertion: "I am about to leave you and expect to see your faces no more. I long to preach to the poor Africans the way of life and salvation. I don't know what may befall me, whether I may find a grave in the ocean, or among the savage men, or more savage wild beasts on the Coast of Africa; nor am I anxious what may become of me. I feel it my duty to go; and I very much fear that many of those who preach the Gospel in this country, will blush when the Saviour calls them to give an account of their labors in His cause and tell them, 'I commanded you to go into all the world, and preach the Gospel to every creature;' . . . the Saviour may ask where have you been? What have you been doing? Have you endeavored to the utmost of your ability to fulfill the commands I gave you, or have you sought your own gratification, and your own ease, regardless of My commands?"[4]

Lott Carey was the first black missionary to sail to Africa and was responsible for planting the first Baptist church in Liberia, which was named the Providence Baptist Church. When he died in 1828 the church had 100 members. In 1830 a revival began and continued for six months extending through the surrounding villages. A hundred more souls were added to the church. The nation of Liberia, Africa's first independent nation, was born in the sanctuary of Providence. The first legislative assembly was held in its sanctuary. It is seen, even today, as the "Cornerstone of the Nation."[5]

Bonnie Witherall

Bonnie and Gary Witherall got married after graduating from Moody Bible Institute in 1997. They settled into the good life in Portland, Oregon. They had it all—money, cars, a house—but there was an emptiness. They knew that God intended them to be doing His work. Their search for ministry opportunities led them to Sidon, Lebanon. These are the words Bonnie wrote in her journal in 2001:

> Lord, here we are in the Middle East. How many people will die in this city of Sidon today without knowing You? How can I worry about my life or Gary's life when tens of thousands of people may die and face eternal damnation today? Lord, my life is already hidden with You. I know You. I have the truth. There is nothing they can take from me.[6]

Bonnie had no way of knowing then that in November 2002 she would be present with her Lord. She loved working at a prenatal clinic with disadvantaged pregnant women. It was a small Christian complex that offered a clinic as well as a chapel, in a high-risk area that served Muslims. As she climbed the stairs to the second-floor clinic she realized that someone was following her. She expected that it was the first person who she would treat in the clinic that morning. Instead it was a gunman who from point-blank range shot her three times in the head. She died instantly.

Her husband, Gary, has spoken across the country encouraging young people to go to the mission field where the harvest is truly plentiful, but the laborers are few. Her life and her death have inspired countless new missionaries to take the gospel to hard places, trusting that God will supply needs and help for the harvest.

These are the words Bonnie wrote in her journal before God

led them to Sidon, Lebanon:

> I don't know what God has for us, but I want to be available to go
> ... I feel like God has me blindfolded and is leading me along a
> path I don't quite understand. But I will follow Him.[7]

I think the Christian life is supposed to be like that, really. We are followers of Christ. We go where He leads us. And He often leads us into places of suffering for the sake of the gospel. But His call is not just for us to be willing to die for the gospel. He calls us to live for it—to take it to the suffering masses who need a Savior.

SUFFERING FOR THE CAUSE OF JUSTICE

In *Woke Church: An Urgent Call for Christians in America to Confront Racism and Injustice,* pastor Eric Mason argues that we have left out a key part of what it means to be followers of Jesus Christ:

> As exiles in this world, we must see ourselves as incarnational
> missionaries in the world for justice. Shalom is the means for
> justice to be done. Jesus said, "Blessed are the peacemakers,
> for they will be called children of God" (Matt. 5:9 NIV). Since
> we are children of God we must be peacemakers. We can't be
> peacemakers and ignore injustice. Ignoring injustice isn't a sign
> of being an authentic believer. Particularly, ignoring systemic
> injustice.[8]

We lost a true warrior in the battle for justice in America recently with the death of Congressman John Lewis. His life was spent on the front lines suffering and fighting for the rights of the poor and the marginalized in this country.

John Robert Lewis

I was privileged to meet and talk with Congressman Lewis several times when he would go to Selma to mark the historic march across the Edmund Pettus Bridge. He would usually speak at a Saturday evening event, and I would preach at one of the church services on the next day.

He came to be known for what happened on the Edmund Pettus Bridge in Selma, Alabama, on March 7, 1965. It's been called one of the most famous marches in American history. Six hundred people were marching for the right to vote. They were brutally beaten by state troopers in what became known as Bloody Sunday. John Lewis's skull was split open by a billy club during the beating.

Lewis was also one of the original Freedom Riders who rode buses through the South, staging sit-ins at lunch counters and demonstrations at department stores. One of the buses was firebombed, and when they ran from the bus they were attacked with baseball bats, iron pipes, and bicycle chains. His unconscious, bloody body was found near a bus terminal in Montgomery, Alabama, and he was repeatedly arrested for nonviolent protests.[9] But in 1961 Attorney General Robert Kennedy banned segregation on buses, and three years later in all public spaces. In 1965 the historic Voting Rights Act was signed.

John Lewis went on to serve as a Congressman in the House of Representatives from 1987 until his death in 2020. His life was spent suffering and sacrificing for the cause of justice. He is a model for believers today who are called to continue the fight for justice until all are treated as equals.

Fannie Lou Hamer

The lament of "Amazing Grace" was a favorite song of my friend Fannie Lou Hamer. She was well acquainted with suffering. She suffered poverty and forced sterilization. When she visited with us in Mendenhall, her words, "I'm just sick and tired of being sick and tired," voiced the mournful lament of her heart.

She lost the job that she had worked tirelessly at for twenty years because she dared to think that blacks should have the right to vote. Instead of going back discouraged, she pushed through her fears and said that when they kicked her off the plantation it was like getting her freedom papers.

She became a community organizer, helping people get registered to vote and tending to the needs of the poor. Her commitment to the civil rights movement was not without a high cost. Over the course of her life, she was repeatedly arrested and beaten. Her arrest in 1963 in Winona, Mississippi, resulted in lifelong injuries from a blood clot in her eye, and permanent kidney damage. But this did not turn her back. She continued the voter registration fight and helped establish the National Women's Political Caucus in 1971.[10]

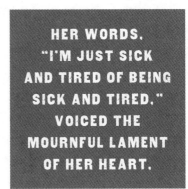

HER WORDS, "I'M JUST SICK AND TIRED OF BEING SICK AND TIRED," VOICED THE MOURNFUL LAMENT OF HER HEART.

Viola Liuzzo

Viola Liuzzo always kept a journal. This is what she wrote when she saw blacks being attacked on the Edmund Pettus Bridge by police dogs and water hoses: "I can't sit back and watch my people suffer." The FBI confiscated her journal and finally returned it to her family. Her daughter said, "She actually believed it when Christ said that the suffering and needy are our people. Mom saw all other human beings as her people."[11]

Viola Liuzzo, a middle-class white wife and mother who was jolted into action when she saw what was happening in the South to blacks who wanted the right to vote. She watched the televised reports of Bloody Sunday and heard the call of Dr. Martin Luther King Jr. She had grown up poor in Chattanooga, Tennessee. She hated what it felt like to be so poor, struggling to survive from day to day. But as bad as it was for her family, she could see that it was even worse for black kids. That realization caused her to look at life differently. It caused her to risk everything to stand up for civil rights and for justice.

She had a lot on the line. She was young, just thirty-nine-years old, and married to a Teamsters agent. She was the mother of five children. She had achieved the American dream. When her husband told her that the fight for civil rights wasn't her fight, she said, "It's everybody's fight!" She asked her best friend, Sara Evans, a black restaurant worker, to care for her children if anything happened to her. And she left her home in Detroit, Michigan, driving to Selma, Alabama, to march for justice.

She had only been in Selma for one week when she lost her life. She volunteered to drive the weary marchers from Montgomery to Selma in her 1963 Oldsmobile. She was spotted by a group of Klansmen who noticed that there was a black man riding her. She was shot twice in the head and was the first white woman to lose her life in the struggle for civil rights.[12] The suffering continued as her family received death threats—shots were fired into their home, and a cross was burned on their lawn. She risked everything and paid the ultimate sacrifice because she cared deeply for the poor. She believed that Jesus meant it when He commanded us to care for the poor.

Saturday Justice in Mississippi

There was a particular Saturday that set me onto the search for justice in Mississippi. It was the Saturday afternoon when my brother Clyde was killed. He had fought in World War II and was wounded in Germany. He came home with battle scars, and we were so proud of him. This particular Saturday he had gone to see a movie. He was waiting at the side entrance of the Caroline Theatre which led to the balcony or "colored section." The marshal, or police chief, "Uncle Bud" Thurman, had a way of walking the streets and coming up behind black people and hitting them on the head with his blackjack. He hit Clyde on the head. When Clyde turned and grabbed the blackjack in self-defense, the marshal stepped back and shot him twice in the stomach. Clyde rode in my arms to the hospital in Jackson and died a few hours after we got there.[13]

> NO AMOUNT OF SUFFERING SHOULD KEEP US FROM MAKING SURE THE DIGNITY OF EVERY HUMAN BEING IS RESPECTED AND AFFIRMED.

These events convinced me that the fight for equal rights was a worthy one. And like John Lewis, Fannie Lou Hamer, and Viola Liuzzo, I saw the right to vote as a crucial right for all people. No amount of suffering should keep us from making sure the dignity of every human being is respected and affirmed. We are all created in His image and likeness.

SUFFERING WITH FELLOW-SUFFERERS

In *The Problem of Pain*, C. S. Lewis said, "Suffering is not good in itself. What is good in any painful experience is, for the sufferer, his submission to the will of God, and, for the spectators, the compassion aroused and the acts of mercy to which it leads."[14]

This may be one of our greatest privileges as believers—to come alongside others who are hurting and bring the balm of healing, comfort, and encouragement. The apostle Paul says in 2 Corinthians 1:4 that God comforts us so that when others hurt we can comfort them with the same comfort we have received from Him. We have freely received His comfort, and we should freely share it with others who desperately need it.

Jesus showed us again and again how important it is to identify with those who are suffering, and to come alongside them in their need. He was moved with compassion when He saw the hunger of the masses who had followed Him. He saw the suffering of those who were demon-possessed and those who suffered from sickness (Matt. 8). He dared to touch a man who was a leper to heal him (Matt. 8:3). He saw the suffering of the woman who had been caught in adultery and refused to condemn her, instead speaking words of peace and encouragement (John 8:3–11). He heard the pain in the ruler's voice as he spoke of his daughter who was dead (Matt. 9:18). On the way to restore her to life, He entered the suffering of a woman who had an issue of blood for twelve long years (Matt. 9:20–22). He saw the suffering of two blind man who cried out to Him for mercy, and He restored their sight (Matt. 9:27–30). He went out of His way to go into Samaritan country to minister to a suffering woman who was an outcast because she had made some poor choices in life. He met her at the well at noon and gave her living water (John 4:7–42).

Suffering people were all around Jesus—literally. Everywhere He turned there was suffering. And He showed us how to suffer with others. He showed us what compassion looks like. He wept with Martha and Mary at Lazarus's tomb (John 11:35). He knew that He was going to raise Lazarus from the dead, but He wept with Martha and Mary. He was *with* them in their suffering.

THEY'VE MADE OUR SUFFERING THEIRS

After her son Matthew's suicide, Kay Warren shared, "This sounds cheesy, but it's the truth that I have received my deepest comfort from God. And we also have some friends who have decided to make our suffering theirs. They have not urged us to get over it, to move on, they've just chosen to suffer alongside of us, and they've moved at our pace."[15]

I think that's the secret of how to suffer with others. It's more listening than talking. It's more sitting with than doing. It's being with them and resisting the pressure to try to make it better.

I've been blessed with a host of friends—true friends—who have come alongside me in my times of suffering. When we received bomb threats during the civil rights movement, hundreds of men came to watch over us at night so that we could sleep. When Vera Mae got so very sick, our friends were there for us. After the loss of our sons

> I THINK THAT'S THE SECRET OF HOW TO SUFFER WITH OTHERS. IT'S MORE LISTENING THAN TALKING. IT'S MORE SITTING WITH THAN DOING.

Spencer and later, Wayne, our friends were there. And during my own bouts with cancer and discouragement, our friends have been there. They listened. They cried with us. They offered a word of encouragement. And most of all they helped us know that we were not alone.

A pastor shared his experience in speaking at a funeral for an infant. The child's father had placed him on a waterbed to take a nap. While he slept he rolled over and suffocated. The parents held hands at the funeral as the father rocked back and forth, sobbing quietly. The pastor realized that his prepared notes were not adequate for the depth of pain in that place. Then he remembered his own grief, just two days ago when his best friend committed suicide, and when the doctors had told him that they weren't able to get all the cancer. He remembered when his little sister died. And he began to weep. Then he spoke, "I can't begin to know your pain right now. I don't even pretend to know the depth of your hurt. But I do know that when I've sat where you're sitting, I doubted God's presence. I asked, 'Where are you, God?'"

The father looked up. He continued speaking, "In the distance, if you will listen, you will hear a voice. Go to the voice. It is saying, 'Come unto me all who are weary and heavy laden, and I will give you rest.' Go to the voice. God is in the voice."[16]

In *Spiritual Friends*, Robert Kelleman describes this as "climbing into the casket" with others as they face daily deaths.[17] The role of a spiritual friend is to share in the misery and the suffering and to provide human comfort. We can do that for our friends who are going through their own Gethsemane. We can help them shoulder the burden, so they are not alone. God uses our own suffering to prepare us to serve one another like this. He comforts us while we are hurting so that we can share that same comfort with others (2 Cor. 1:4).

Paul David Tripp reminds us that our sufferings don't even belong to us, they belong to the Lord. He will "take hard and difficult things in your life and use them to produce good things in the lives of others. This is one of the unexpected miracles of his grace."[18]

When I wrote *He Calls Me Friend: The Healing Power of Friendship in a Lonely World*, this is the kind of friendship I had in mind. The world is full of hurting people. This has always been true. But especially now, because of the coronavirus, the hurt, suffering, and loneliness have been multiplied. There is no end to the opportunities we have to love one another and to support one another.

CHAPTER SIX

In His Steps

*"But how is it to your credit if you receive a beating for doing wrong
and endure it? But if you suffer for doing good and you endure it,
this is commendable before God. To this you were called, because Christ
suffered for you, leaving you an example, that you should follow in his steps.
'He committed no sin, and no deceit was found in his mouth.'
When they hurled their insults at him, he did not retaliate;
when he suffered, he made no threats.
Instead, he entrusted himself to him who judges justly."*

1 PETER 2:20–23

These verses served as the basis for *In His Steps*, a classic written by Charles Sheldon. It tells the story of Henry Maxwell, the proud pastor of First Church, the most prestigious and wealthy church in the area. While the pastor was working through his message on 1 Peter 2:20–23 and concentrating on his final point on what it means to live a life of sacrifice and follow Jesus' example, a poor man knocked at his door. He was asking for help finding a job. Pastor Maxwell was annoyed at the disturbance and turned him away. The poor man went next door to the church building and was turned away there as well. The next day was Sunday, and as the pastor preached his fine sermon on sacrificing for others, the same man walked down the aisle of the church. He looked at the congregation and explained that his wife had died four months ago, and he was trying to provide for his small child. He had come to the church looking for help and found none. He asked the congregation what it meant to follow in Jesus' steps. Did they really mean the words they had just sung, "Where He leads me I will follow"?

The congregation listened in stunned silence. The poor man collapsed in front of the church and died a few days later. That event moved the pastor to challenge the church members to ask themselves one question for the next year before they made any decisions: *What would Jesus do?* [1]

That one question transformed the lives of every member of that congregation who accepted the challenge. Bankers found themselves lending to people they would normally reject. People found themselves going the extra mile to help people they would normally ignore. The church was transformed, and so was the town.

It's believed that Peter wrote the epistle that Maxwell preached from around AD 65 as the followers of Christ were moving into a period of persecution. The Romans had tolerated Christianity because they thought it was a subgroup of Judaism. But when it became clear that they were distinct from Judaism, it was no longer considered an approved state religion. [2] They were now subject to fierce persecution by the Roman authorities. In his letter, Peter emphasized the sufferings of believers and the sufferings of Christ. He encouraged them to remain steadfast and faithful. Believers in the early church were so committed to this truth that "at the Nicene Council, an important church meeting in the 4th century A.D., of the 318 delegates attending, fewer than 12 had not lost an eye or or lost a hand or lost a hand or did not limp on a leg lamed by torture for their Christian faith."[3]

SUFFERING AND DOING GOOD

Here's where I rejoice. We get to follow Jesus' example in suffering! His suffering was not just for Him. It was meant to show you and me how we should suffer. Peter says that God is pleased when we do good and suffer for it with patience. What is the "doing good" that God expects of us? Jesus talked a lot about that in His Sermon on the Mount. This is what He's looking for from those of us who are His children:

- *Turn the other cheek:* swallow your pride and walk away rather than risk confrontation that could result in hurt to the other person or loss of life.

- *Give to the person who is suing you:* be willing to suffer loss rather than to damage your witness by being taken to court.

- *Go the extra mile:* it was accepted practice in Roman-occupied territory for soldiers to command citizens to carry their burdens or belongings for one mile. Jesus wanted His followers to demonstrate generosity by offering to go even further than expected.

- *Give to the person who asks of you:* you have received freely from Him and should give freely to those who ask of you.

- *Love your enemies:* refuse to hate; instead look for opportunities to bless and extend kindness to those who do not like you.

- *Speak well of those who curse you:* it's not enough to not return curse for curse. We should speak kindly about those who curse us.

- *Do good to those who hate you:* look for opportunities to bless your enemies.

- *Pray for your persecutors:* ask God to bless and have mercy on your enemies.

When I was young I wasn't thinking like this. I grew up rough. We ran afoul of the law a lot. And still today, I have a lot of dark spots in my life. The Lord is still showing me dark spots. But that's His love for me. He's trying to wash off all my spots so when I see Him in heaven I'll be pure. It is the outworking of His life. I want to honor Him in that. I think that's where the joy is. When He shows up in me, I find myself doing things that in my flesh I would not normally do. I find myself loving enemies and praying for those who don't like me. But I want to be careful to not steal His glory in this. None of this is me. I'm still in need of fixing in so many ways. All of us are. But He keeps teaching us and bringing us along.

CHOOSE THE RIGHT SIDE

The enemy of our souls has made it really easy for believers in America to choose the way of ease and self-preservation. He has lulled many of us to sleep on beds of comfort and wealth. We are satisfied with ourselves. Pleased with ourselves and all that we have accomplished. But I think He calls us to enter the suffering of other people. Henri Nouwen calls that "passion." He suggests that "compassion is hard because it requires the inner disposition to go with others to the place where they are weak, vulnerable, lonely, and broken. But this is not our spontaneous response to suffering. What we desire most is to do away with suffering by fleeing from it or finding a quick cure for it."[4]

But our Lord calls us to do for others what He did for us. He left His home in glory and came to live among sinful people so that He could die for us and make a way for us to be with Him forever. I think He's saying to us, "I suffered for you. Now I want you to join me in the mission to the lost and the broken." That's what discipleship is. That's the mission! And we need to make a choice, just like the Good Samaritan.

> **WHEN I READ THE PARABLE OF THE GOOD SAMARITAN, I WONDER WHICH ONE OF THE PEOPLE I WOULD HAVE BEEN LIKE.**

When I read the parable of the Good Samaritan I wonder which one of the people I would have been like. A Jewish man had been robbed and badly beaten on the road from Jerusalem to Jericho. He was left to die. By chance a religious leader, a priest, came upon him. He looked and walked to the other side of the road. Then a Levite came upon the man. The Levites were those who assisted the priests in the worship in the Jewish temple. He looked and walked to the other side of the road as well. Finally, a Samaritan approached. He bandaged the man's wounds and took him to get help, promising to return and pay whatever amount was needed for the man's care.

The two religious people walked away, showing no compassion on their fellow brother. But the Samaritan, who was seen as unclean by Jews, showed mercy and compassion. He was the true neighbor in Jesus' parable.

With all that is going on in our world today, we are faced with these kinds of choices every day. Every time we turn on the television we see images of hurting people. There is so much suffering that we can almost become numb to it. We can choose to extend ourselves to those who are hurting, or we can look away and pretend that it is not our problem.

Joshua in the Old Testament and Jesus in the New Testament both challenge us to think carefully about the choice we make:

"Now fear the LORD and serve him with all faithfulness. . . . But if serving the LORD seems undesirable to you, then choose for yourselves this day whom you will serve. . . . But as for me and my household, we will serve the LORD" (Josh. 24:14a–15).

"No one can serve two masters. Either you will hate the one and love the other, or you will be devoted to the one and despise the other. You cannot serve both God and money" (Matt. 6:24).

We get to choose whether the things of God are worth suffering for. Discipleship demands that we choose service to Christ, for the good of others and for His glory.

GIVE SACRIFICIALLY

My heart is moved when I see so many people who are struggling to survive and are on the verge of being put out of their homes. We can give to churches and organizations who are helping provide for these needs. And if we know some of these people personally we can give directly to them. If every one of us gives at least a little, then many can be fed and kept safe.

Maybe this issue of hunger hits so close to home for me because I grew up suffering from poverty. I remember too well what it was like to be hungry. And I remember how being poor and on the lowest rung of society can drain you of hope and purpose. It can kill your soul.

I was confronted with the ugliness of being poor when I was twelve years old. I had worked all day hauling hay in the fields of a white farmer. I expected to be paid at least a dollar, or maybe two, for my work. When it came time to be paid I was given fifteen cents—a dime and a buffalo head nickel. I couldn't demand to be paid a fair wage—I was only a child and I was black. But I felt the sting of poverty and the heaviness of it all in that moment. I saw it reflected in the faces of other people who looked down on me, and I felt it deep in my soul. Poverty is a suffering that goes deep. And it still stretches far and wide across our country.

America is a land of plenty. Even in the midst of a pandemic and loss of jobs, this is still a land of plenty. The problem is that the people who have plenty don't want to share it with those who desperately need it. This is Discipleship 101, caring for the poor. Jesus said, "For I was hungry and you gave me something to eat, I was thirsty and you gave me something to drink, I was a stranger and you invited me in, I needed clothes and you clothed me, I was sick and you looked after me, I was in prison and you came to visit me" (Matt. 25:35–36).

On the issue of giving, C. S. Lewis said this: "I do not believe one can settle how much we ought to give. I am afraid the only safe rule is to give more than we can spare."[5] And this story is told of the Spurgeons' generosity:

Charles Spurgeon and his wife, Susie, according to a story in *The Chaplain* magazine, would sell, but refused to give away, the eggs their chickens laid. Even close relatives were told, "You may have them if you pay for them." As a result, some people labeled the Spurgeons greedy and grasping.

They accepted the criticisms without defending themselves, and only after Mrs. Spurgeon died was the full story revealed. All the profits from the sale of eggs went to support two elderly widows. Because the Spurgeons were unwilling to let their left hand know what the right hand was doing (Matthew 6:3), they endured the attacks in silence.[6]

So yes, the Lord calls us to give out of our abundance and even out of our lack. But He also calls us to forgive, even when it hurts.

A JAIL IN PHILIPPI

When the apostle Paul cast a demon out of a young woman in Philippi, he got the chance to suffer for doing good (Acts 16:16–39). Her masters were angry because they made money off her. They took Paul and Silas to the marketplace and demanded that they be beaten. They were badly beaten and thrown into prison. The keeper of the prison had them locked in the lowest part of the prison. Most of us would probably have been angry right about then. We would probably be complaining and depressed. But at midnight Paul and Silas were singing and praising God for the privilege of suffering for Him. That's a lesson right there! It's a privilege to do good and suffer for it. That's something to praise God for.

That's what Paul and Silas were doing when God shook the jail with an earthquake, loosing all their chains. They were free! Free to walk away and tend to their wounds. Free to walk away from that place of suffering. And the jailer expected them to do that. He drew his sword to take his own life because he would be held responsible for letting them escape. But Paul stopped him. He assured him that they were still there. And what happened next is what I shout about. The former enemy became a brother in Christ, as the jailer asked, "Sirs, what must I do to be saved?" (Acts 16:30). Paul shared the glorious news of the gospel with him, and his whole household became believers. This new brother in Christ began washing the wounds of Paul and Silas. I love that picture. Paul shows us what can happen when we refuse to strike back against our enemies. When we choose to suffer *with rejoicing* a door is opened for the gospel to be shared. That, my friend, is joy!

When I tell that story now it sticks with people. Real reconciliation is washing the wounds that we cause each other. When Paul wrote to the Philippians, his letter was so personal because they came together around suffering. He was saying to them, "You are my joy, and you are my rejoicing. We came together in pain and I became a prisoner of Jesus Christ for the rest of my life. But you are my joy. You are my reward. You are my rejoicing. So, rejoice in the Lord always . . . and again I say, rejoice!"

ANOTHER JAIL . . .

I've had some of my own jailhouse suffering. And God showed up there too. He didn't come in an

> **REAL RECONCILIATION IS WASHING THE WOUNDS THAT WE CAUSE EACH OTHER.**

earthquake, but He showed up and helped me see that my heart was locked in its own prison of anger and bitterness. It was 1970. We had led a successful boycott to help people who were suffering from poverty see the power they had when they stopped buying from businesses that didn't respect them. When two vanloads of students who had worked with our ministry were arrested, we rushed to the jail to help them. I didn't know that they were being used to lure me into the jail.

When I got there, I was beaten almost to death. My head was battered, bludgeoned, and bloodied by a mob of policemen, whose rage had no limits. I lost consciousness and my body went numb. But through the haze of semiconsciousness I saw them as they were—as much captive to their racism and bigotry as I was to the walls of the prison. And I was aware of the hatred in my own heart toward them. If I could have, I probably would have thrown a grenade into that jail and killed everybody. We were all captives. All sufferers. And in that dark, bloody place, that's where He showed up. He gave me eyes to see that the darkness of their hearts was matched by the hatred in my own heart. I was desperate to get out of there before they killed me. He released me from that prison of torture, but that was just the beginning of how He intended to set me free.

It was the Tufts Medical Center in Mound Bayou where He showed up again. This was a black hospital in an all-black town. The hospital was run down and had been revived so they had a place to use during the civil rights movement. It was there where nurses and doctors—both white and black—were volunteering their time to help. My body was broken, and my spirit was crushed. I was discouraged, and I was angry. This was my true Gethsemane. The desire for revenge was so strong it almost overwhelmed me. But He used a black doctor, Dr. Harvey Sanders, who operated on me and reminded me that there were black people who were committed to people and their needs. And he used a white Catholic doctor, Dr. Joann Roberts, who bandaged and healed my wounds. She would talk to me and give me a sense of hope. And over time my heart began to melt, as layers of resistance fell away.

The choice was set before me. There was a clear line drawn between the nonviolent resistance of Dr. Martin Luther King Jr. and the radical Black Power of Malcolm X. The temptation of the enemy and of my flesh to hate white people was great. But there was no peace in my heart when I thought of revenge. It was only when I chose to love that peace flooded my soul. He taught me to see them as fellow sufferers. The rage that marked their faces—I wanted to match it with a love that was just as radical, just as revolutionary. I came to understand that the only way for blacks to be freed from the shackles of racism was for whites to be freed from the same shackles.[7] We were handcuffed and leg-ironed together. I think Dr. King said it best: "our destinies are tied together. And somehow we must learn to live together as brothers in this country or we're all going to perish together as fools."[8]

This didn't happen overnight. It took some time for my heart and my body to heal. I had learned to hate white folks early in life. And learning forgiveness and love took time. But He got me there. He showed me how to love. And I came to know a different kind of suffering. I think what happens when you are beaten and tortured and then become famous is that you begin to think that you deserve that fame. You become the victim of your own self-importance. People are drawn to you because of what happened, and your motivation can get twisted. I've had to battle against the temptation to feel like everything that came to me was deserved. None of it was. It was God's hand of blessing.

Being beaten for doing right is hard. It's tempting to fight back and to hate back. But Jesus' example teaches all of us how to really love those who cause us to suffer. When we suffer without striking back we look like Him.

This parable inspires me:

A holy man was engaged in his morning meditation under a tree whose roots stretched out over the riverbank. During his meditation he noticed that the river was rising, and a scorpion caught in the roots was about to drown. He crawled out on the roots and reached down to free the scorpion, but every time he did so, the scorpion struck back at him. An observer came along and said to the holy man, "Don't you know that's a scorpion, and it's in the nature of a scorpion to want to sting?" To which the holy man replied, "That may well be, but it is my nature to save, and must I change my nature because the scorpion does not change its nature?"[9]

Our enemies may never change; but it's in our nature to love, to forgive, to suffer for and with other hurting souls, to model the heart of Christ. When we do that—fighting back our fleshly desires for revenge and submitting to the Holy Spirit in us to love—that's joy!

CHAPTER SEVEN

Deal with Fear

"There is no fear in love. But perfect love drives out fear . . . "

1 JOHN 4:18A

There's a huge barrier that keeps us from choosing suffering, whether it's for the advance of the gospel, for the cause of justice, or to identify with others who suffer. That barrier is fear. We're afraid. Our culture has been carried away by fear of the "other." People who don't look like us, or vote like us, or think like us have become demonized. Some of us are afraid of the people at our southern border, or progressive liberals, or violence in our streets. Others of us are afraid of right-wing conservatives, or the police, or hate groups. We're afraid of the changing demographics of our neighborhoods. We're afraid. The result is that we are frozen in our fear.

According to the YouVersion Bible App, the most-read Bible verse for 2020 was Isaiah 41:10: "So do not fear, for I am with you; do not be dismayed, for I am your God. I will strengthen you and help you; I will uphold you with my righteous right hand." The app was searched almost six hundred million times, with fear, healing, and justice ranked as the most-searched topics.[1]

FEAR IS REAL

The Lord knew that one of the enemy's main weapons would be fear. From the very beginning, Satan used it to convince Adam and Eve to doubt and question whether God really had their best interests at heart. Again and again in Scripture, whenever the Lord's messenger interacted with a human being his first words were "Fear not!" These words appear more than 365 times throughout Scripture. That lets us know that fear is not uncommon. It's human to fear.

It's important to remember that not all fear is bad. Good fear is reverence and awe for God. But when He says, "fear not," He's talking about the kind of fear that cripples us and keeps us from obeying His call to love and serve others. Everyone who God used in the Bible had to deal with their fears. I'm grateful that the stories in the Bible left that part in. When I see what the heroes of our faith accomplished, they seem almost superhuman. It helps to know that they had to deal with their own fears too. Just like we do.

Gideon was afraid and put God to the test repeatedly (Judg. 6:17–23). The disciples were afraid when the stormy water of the Sea of Galilee whipped against their boat at night (Mark 4:35–41). Peter made bold claims about dying for Jesus, even if everybody else turned away. And before midnight he had denied knowing Jesus three times—because of fear (Luke 22:57–60).

In *Love over Fear*, Dan White Jr. shares his personal journey through fear. With raw honesty, he talks about taking a leisurely walk through his neighborhood and seeing a black man. Immediately he became afraid. Just the image of a black man in his neighborhood struck fear in his heart. The fear was not based on anything the young man had done. It was based on a prejudgment. Those prejudgments keep us sheltered in our neighborhoods, afraid to cross the tracks where "they" live. We're afraid to have conversations about justice because we might say the wrong thing. We're afraid to take a stand because we might lose friendships with people who are in our group. We're afraid.

HIS WORD FOR OUR FEARS

How often I have found shelter and comfort in the strength of His Word in my times of fear and anxiety. There is power in the Word. Here's how He speaks to our fears:

- "God is our refuge and strength, an ever-present help in trouble" (Ps. 46:1).

- "The LORD is with me; I will not be afraid. What can mere mortals do to me? The LORD is with me; he is my helper" (Ps. 118:6–7).

- "Fear of man will prove to be a snare, but whoever trusts in the LORD is kept safe" (Prov. 29:25).

- "The angel of the LORD encamps around those who fear him, and he delivers them" (Ps. 34:7).

- "The LORD is my light and my salvation—whom shall I fear? The LORD is the stronghold of my life—of whom shall I be afraid?" (Ps. 27:1)

- "When I am afraid, I put my trust in you" (Ps. 56:3).

- "Peace I leave with you; my peace I give you. I do not give to you as the world gives. Do not let your hearts be troubled and do not be afraid" (John 14:27).

- "Do not be anxious about anything, but in every situation, by prayer and petition, with thanksgiving, present your requests to God. And the peace of God, which transcends all understanding, will guard your hearts and your minds in Christ Jesus" (Phil. 4:6–7).

Let's meditate on these precious promises. He will keep us when we make up our minds to reach across the divide, to love people who don't look like us, to cherish the image of God in the face of every person we meet. He will give us courage to break away from that hate group or to speak up when someone makes a racist, ugly statement.

THIS WE KNOW

When Captain Sullenberger (Sully) landed US Airways Flight 1549 on the Hudson River on January 15, 2009, he was asked if he was afraid. Almost immediately after the flight took off from New York's LaGuardia Airport it hit a flock of geese and went down. All of the 155 passengers on the flight were rescued, and very few had serious injuries. Sully had been a trainer, teaching pilots how to land on water if a plane went down. But he didn't take credit for saving those people on that flight. He managed his fear because of his knowledge. The flight attendants did what they were taught to do. They drew on their knowledge, and everybody survived the miracle landing. But it was what they all knew that controlled their fear.

When we think about suffering with those who are hurting, it's human to fear. *What if I get hurt? What if I get sick? What if something happens to me?* What we *know* should help to keep our fear under control. We know that all things work together for those who love the Lord and are called according to His purposes (Rom. 8:28). We know this. We know that when we suffer, we identify with Him. And we know that He is with us always. This we know.

When we are afraid, we don't have to pretend that we are not. We can say, "God, I'm afraid." Courage isn't the absence of fear. I think courage is propelled by fear. The hero is the one who forgets about himself in the moment and does what needs to be done. Heroes jump into the river to save someone, knowing that they may die, but they also may rescue that person. And they reckon in that split second that it's a sacrifice worth making.

In my book *Dream with Me*, I talked about the fear so many parents felt when our children decided they were going to integrate the movie theater in Mendenhall. It was 1964, and our four oldest children were a part of the group. The children all knew that they would likely be taken to jail and beaten up, so they tried their best to keep it a secret from their parents. The parents were not only afraid for their children, they all risked losing their jobs, their homes, and their insurance if their children went to jail for trying to integrate a whites-only facility. In spite of the great risk, I was so proud that our children were willing to give their lives to the cause. As it turned out, the theater owners must have gotten word of the protest because they closed the theater—permanently.[2]

I was overwhelmed with fear when I drove my car up to the jail in Brandon in 1970. When I saw the twelve patrolmen rushing from the jail toward us I knew that we had been set up. I never expected them to come out to the car and start beating us without reason. I never expected that. And the fear was

> HE'S CALLING US TO SUFFER WITH THOSE WHO ARE HURTING AND TO LAY OUR LIVES ON THE LINE FOR THE CAUSE OF JUSTICE. WE CAN'T LET FEAR KEEP US FROM ANSWERING THE CALL.

immediate and overwhelming. I knew things were going to get bad. But there was nothing I could do to stop what was happening. I had to cry out to the Lord. And He was with me. He kept me in spite of my fears.

I think all of us are afraid at some level about what has been happening in our country recently. The coronavirus took over the entire world and racial strife is getting worse every day. Fires have scorched large parts of the Western states. And hurricanes seem to be coming faster and fiercer every season. This may be the one time that God is speaking to all of us at the same time. He's speaking to the rich, the poor, the educated, the uneducated, black, white, Hispanic—every one of us. I think He's calling us out of the world, calling us to stand for truth, for what is right. Calling us to suffer with those who are hurting and to lay our lives on the line for the cause of justice. We can't let fear keep us from answering the call.

I agree with the challenge in this message on fear by John Piper:

> I call you to recognize that God is greater than your personality. God is greater than your past experiences of timidity. God is greater than your "family of origin." And God calls you to joyful fearlessness. The crucial factor in your fearless living is not your family but your God. *Let not your hearts be troubled, believe in God.*

Believe in God! Trust God! Let God be your God! Your help. Your strength. He will uphold you with his righteous right hand.[3]

THEY'LL KNOW WE ARE CHRISTIANS BY OUR LOVE

Love is the hallmark of the children of God. "By this everyone will know that you are my disciples, if you love one another" (John 13:35). The world will know Him when it sees His children displaying uncommon, sacrificial love. If that is true, then we must learn how to conquer our fears and love the unlovable, forgive the unforgivable. And my joy is that I don't have to strive and try to figure out what this love looks like. It's His love that He pours out on me. I'm supposed to be a channel of blessing and love to everyone I come in contact with.

This love answers the age-old question: how should we then live? I think that means we should live as the hands and feet of Christ. We should love the people He would love; help the people He would help—and even be willing to die for our enemies—just like Jesus did for us.

The Good Samaritan story challenges each of us with a bold question: will we be a neighbor? Will we be inconvenienced by the pain and suffering of someone else? Will we put our prejudices aside to care about the hurts of someone who doesn't look like us? Are we willing to suffer loss for the sake of someone else?

In a split second Wesley Autrey made the decision to risk loss for a stranger. Five years after his heroic effort, he said, "I think God has a calling for me."[4] On that morning Wesley, a black construction worker, and his two daughters were on the 137th Street subway platform in New York waiting for a train. He was taking his girls to school on his way to work. He observed twenty-year-old Cameron Hollopeter having a seizure. He lost his balance and ended up down on the tracks. When Wesley looked up and saw the #1 train approaching and heard the horn blowing, he knew the conductor would not have time to stop the train. He jumped onto the tracks on top of Cameron, pushing him down in the small twelve-inch space between the rails. Just enough to allow the train to pass over them with less than one inch to spare. Both men survived.

I do believe God has a calling on Wesley Autrey's life. And I believe He has a calling on each of our lives. He calls us to make that split-second sacrifice of life and limb for the sake of others. To make that deliberate choice to love extravagantly and with abandon—to cast fear aside. And He promises that this kind of love destroys fear: "There is no fear in love. But perfect love drives out fear" (1 John 4:18a).

PART THREE

JOY COMES IN THE MORNING

CHAPTER EIGHT

He Can Redeem It All!

*Consider it pure joy, my brothers and sisters, whenever you face trials
of many kinds, because you know that the testing of your faith
produces perseverance. Let perseverance finish its work
so that you may be mature and complete, not lacking anything.*

JAMES 1:2–4

If James, the New Testament writer, is correct, it is possible
to have genuine joy, pure joy, even while we are dealing with
some real hard stuff. Most of his readers had been forced to
leave their homes because of religious persecution, and they were
suffering from extreme poverty. His encouragement to them was
to remind them that God was using their very personal struggles
to test their faith and produce something glorious. The word for
"testing" points back to the process of how gold and silver were
refined. They were placed into the refiner's fire. The heat from the
fire melted the gold and silver to a liquid substance. The impuri-
ties would rise to the top and could be burned off. What was left
was pure gold or pure silver. It's said that the silversmith would

keep putting the silver back into the fire until he was able to see his own reflection in it.

This is what suffering does for each of us. It puts us into the refiner's fire so that we can come out looking like Him. It reminds me of the lyrics "Please be patient with me, / God is not through with me yet. / ...when God gets through with me, / ... I shall come forth like pure gold."[1]

I think a lot about how God redeems the suffering of His children. At the end of it all, Job knew God in a way that he could never have known Him without suffering deeply. This knowledge of God is precious. And it is this that He offers to each of us as we suffer. I find so much comfort and so much joy in this reality.

> A. Parnell Bailey visited an orange grove where an irrigation pump had broken down. The season was unusually dry and some of the trees were beginning to die for lack of water. The man giving the tour then took Bailey to his own orchard where irrigation was used sparingly. "These trees could go without rain for another two weeks," he said. "You see, when they were young, I frequently kept water from them. This hardship caused them to send their roots deeper into the soil in search of moisture. Now mine are the deepest-rooted trees in the area. While others are being scorched by the sun, these are finding moisture at a greater depth."[2]

This is the great paradox of suffering! Suffering drives us deeper in Him. Suffering drives the roots of our faith deep, deep into the reservoir of His sufficiency. With each new privilege to suffer, our roots go even deeper in Him. And before you know it we have become like the tree that David spoke of in Psalm 1. We become "like a tree planted by streams of water, which yields its fruit in season and whose leaf does not wither—whatever they do prospers" (Ps. 1:3). Not only are we strengthened to ready ourselves for the next storm, we produce fruit that shelters, nourishes, and encourages others.

I believe that's what the apostle Paul had in mind when he said, "I want to know Christ— yes, to know the power of his resurrection and participation in his sufferings, becoming like him in his death" (Phil. 3:10). Can there be any higher purpose for

> **SUFFERING DRIVES THE ROOTS OF OUR FAITH DEEP, DEEP INTO THE RESERVOIR OF HIS SUFFICIENCY.**

suffering than to make us rich in Him and ready for eternity? I don't think anything compares to knowing Him with a faith that is unshakeable. He redeems our suffering. He makes much of our suffering in our own lives, and in the lives of others who are watching and deciding whether it's worth it or not to suffer for Him.

NEW CALLINGS, NEW MINISTRY

In that place where you feel hollow and empty, like you have lost everything—something of self dies. And I believe this is where He places new calling and purpose in our hearts. Our suffering has sensitized us to things we knew nothing about before, and we cannot unsee what we have seen. We cannot unhear what we have heard.

The first generation of our people who came out of slavery were responsible for the greatest growth of black churches and black colleges this nation has ever known. They had experienced such deep suffering, and God had birthed from their struggles a burning passion for Him and for learning. Methodist and Baptist churches and denominations sprang up all over the country, as freed slaves were finally able to worship God openly and in their own way. This was the generation that built Howard University, Morehouse College, Hampton University, Fisk University, and many other historically black colleges and universities (HBCUs). Out of much suffering God birthed calling and purpose. If freed slaves could accomplish so very much, with so little, how much more should we be accountable for today?

During the Jim Crow years many black women in the South suffered the loss of their husbands and sons to lynchings and to incarceration. Others saw injustice all around them and ached for true change. This deep, deep pain birthed in them a yearning for justice. Many of them became lawyers and judges out of a desire to change the criminal justice system. One of those young women was Constance Slaughter, the first black woman to graduate from the University of Mississippi Law School. She had just graduated when our case against the Mississippi Highway Patrol was coming together. She joined with the Lawyers' Committee for Civil Rights that was formed by President John Kennedy to help fight cases in the South. She felt that God had called her to speak for those who couldn't speak for themselves.

The Lawyers' Committee sued the state of Mississippi, and because of that legal action blacks were allowed access to positions as highway patrolmen. Two years later Walter Crosby, Lewis Younger, and R. O. Williams became the first African-Americans to serve as highway patrolmen for the state of Mississippi. Constance's life theme is: to whom much is given, much is required. She had no way of knowing how her life would inspire so many other young black girls, like my daughter Joannie and so many others, to believe that they could become lawyers too. Out of much suffering, God birthed callings for His purposes.

COVID-19 stripped many of us down to our core and caused us to consider what is really important in life. Lots of people had never been poor before, and after having to stand in lines waiting for food they will now have a heart for the poor. They'll have a new perspective on how easy it is to become poor through no fault of your own. Churches have been forced to take another look at how we do ministry. Maybe we have been too bound up in the four walls of our buildings. God has forced us into our homes and communities. Perhaps He intends for us to birth ministry that meets the needs of our neighbors in a new way.

The refining fire of suffering is how He breaks us—so He can reshape us, point us in a different direction, and use us for His glory. Whether suffering has chosen us or we have chosen suffering, God can redeem it. And when He does—the glory is all His!

GIVE HIM THE GLORY!

We can count it all joy when He shows up in all His glory at our moments of great despair. The fact that we have not lost our minds, or destroyed ourselves, or utterly given up is proof of His awesome power to keep us! We don't serve a dead God. He is real! Real in the world. Real in my soul.

There's a story of a man who was searching for the perfect picture of peace. Artists from across the globe submitted their masterpieces to the contest. The day came for the winning submission to be revealed. They gasped at the sight of the chosen drawing. In it a waterfall roared over the side of a rocky mountain.

Storm clouds filled the sky and lightning shot across the horizon. Yet one spindly tiny tree stuck out from the side of the mountain through the falls. And perched on one of its branches was a bird. Her arms were spread to shelter her little ones, and her eyes were closed in sweet contentment.[3]

That, my friend, is a picture of the kind of peace that He provides in the midst of the storm. Our suffering is His opportunity to show His power to keep us. Only God can give His child that kind of peace amid pandemics, unrest, chaos, and confusion. He's bigger than all of it.

> **THE FACT THAT WE HAVE NOT LOST OUR MINDS, OR DESTROYED OURSELVES, OR UTTERLY GIVEN UP IS PROOF OF HIS AWESOME POWER TO KEEP US!**

My friend David Kinnaman, president of Barna Research, lost his wife, Jill, to brain cancer not long ago. At her memorial service, person after person spoke of her strength and resolve through the four-year journey. When David, or one of the children, or a friend would be at the point of despair, she was the encourager, always reminding them that God had the power to step in at any moment and miraculously heal her. But if He chose not to do so, she was ready to be with Him. And her testimony of faith pointed everyone who saw her to Him. They saw Him in her suffering. So I would encourage you to ask yourself: *how is He showing up in my suffering right now? Is His power on display? Is His comfort on display?*

It's something to be able to say, "After all I've been through, I still have joy." I pray that you are able to say that. That's a testimony to God's faithfulness and goodness. When it is all said and done, I am grateful for my sufferings. I have been blessed to live long enough to be able to look back and see how the Lord was able to use the very things that the enemy intended to cripple me and make me useless for the kingdom. Instead of being the end of me, the Lord used those things to open doors of service and strengthen my faith. And oh, the doors that He has opened over the course of my lifetime!

We are not limited by what we can do or by who we know. His sufficiency becomes more than enough. That's joy! The apostle Paul said it best: "Therefore I will boast all the more gladly about my weaknesses, so that Christ's power may rest on me. That is why, for Christ's sake, I delight in weaknesses, in insults, in hardships, in persecutions, in difficulties. For when I am weak, then I am strong" (2 Cor. 12:9b–10).

I believe that God redeems our suffering. He reclaims it for His purposes. He uses the things that set us apart and make us unique to prepare us for the work He intends for us to do. And especially, He uses the ways in which we are broken. He can use that brokenness to develop a tender heart for others who are suffering like we are. And in that I do rejoice! There is no waste of tears or suffering. He brings it all together in service to His purposes, because of His great love for us. And there is no greater joy in this life than knowing that every tear matters. Somehow He works it all together in His master plan to produce beauty and joy from ashes.

> David, a 2-year old with leukemia, was taken by his mother, Deborah, to Massachusetts General Hospital in Boston, to see Dr. John Truman who specializes in treating children with cancer and various blood diseases. The prognosis was devastating: "He

has a 50-50 chance." . . . When he was three, he had to have a spinal tap—a painful procedure at any age. It was explained to him that, because he was sick, Dr. Truman had to do something to make him better. "If it hurts, remember it's because he loves you," Deborah said. The procedure was horrendous. It took three nurses to hold David still, while he yelled and sobbed and struggled. When it was almost over, the tiny boy, soaked in sweat and tears, looked up at the doctor and gasped, "Thank you, Dr. Tooman, for my hurting."[4]

Like little David, the apostle Paul gloried in his tribulations because he knew they were all part of God's good plan and would work out for His glory: "Not only so, but we also glory in our sufferings, because we know that suffering produces perseverance" (Rom. 5:3).

At ninety years of age I can finally say, like David and like the apostle Paul, "Thank You, Lord, for my suffering. Thank You for the storms You brought me through. Thank You for every tear that has been shed. Thank You for Your watchful eye that knew just how much I could bear. I rejoice in all that You have done. Thank You, Lord, for my hurting."

CHAPTER NINE

My Eyes Are Fixed

And let us run with perseverance the race marked out for us,
fixing our eyes on Jesus, the pioneer and perfecter of faith.
For the joy set before him he endured the cross, scorning its shame,
and sat down at the right hand of the throne of God.

HEBREWS 12:1B–2

When we suffer it can be all-consuming. It can sap all your strength and keep you in a prison of pain. But I'm pressing through my pain. I am confident that what lies ahead is so much better than anything I've ever known. My eyes are fixed on one thing. My Savior waits for me to finish my race. And that is inexpressible joy!

Hebrews 12 follows the chapter that has been called the Hall of Faith. The writer calls the roll of saints who have gone before us and who now make up the grand audience who cheer us on. They are described as those who: "were tortured, refusing to be released so that they might gain an even better resurrection. Some faced jeers and flogging, and even chains and imprisonment. They were put to death by stoning; they were sawed in two; they were killed by the sword. They went about in sheepskins and goatskins, destitute, persecuted and mistreated—the world was not worthy of them. They wandered in deserts and mountains, living in caves and in holes in the ground" (Heb. 11:35b–38). Their triumph over the pain of this life says to us, "Go on! Keep running! You can make it! You can make it!"

In the ancient Olympic games, the track was an oval or an ellipse, so the beginning point was also the goal. It's interesting that the writer of Hebrews would use this picture to illustrate our faith. It is a perfect picture because Jesus is our beginning and He is our ending. We start our journey of faith resting in the truth that He is who the Bible says He is. "Being confident of this, that he who began a good work in you will carry it on to completion until the day of Christ Jesus" (Phil. 1:6). And we end trusting that it is all true and it will all carry us into eternity. The word used for author is *archegos*, which means pioneer. He has already gone before us and shown us the way. He has marked out our territory. He set the limits on how Satan could test me, just like He did with Job. He has set the limits on how Satan can test you too. I trust Him. And I rejoice that He counted me worthy to endure the things I have experienced.

Life is so much like a race. But it's not a sprint. It's a marathon. If you've given your life to Jesus, you're in it for the duration. Every one of us has to run our own race, the race that is set before us. No one else can run my race for me. No one can run your race for you. All the difficulties, sorrows, losses, and joys were written into your story even before you were born. I believe that He did that for everyone who belongs to Him. He is the author. And He is the finisher.

Marathon runners talk a lot about hitting a wall when they're running. It's the point in the race where the runner's stored energy is depleted and there's nothing left to draw from other than sheer willpower. It's a sudden attack of fatigue; the legs lose all strength. But if the runner can push through, they report getting a new burst of energy and strength to complete the race. Suffering can be like that wall. You can be running your race at a good speed, and suddenly you are hit with calamity. It threatens to take your breath away and make you stop in your tracks.

In 1965 Ronald Melzack and Patrick Wall suggested that if a person can focus on something outside of their pain, it can lessen their suffering. They called this the Gate Control Theory.[1] Their idea was that pain is transmitted through a gate in the dorsal horn of the spinal cord. If those nerves received different input, the pain would be minimized. So, they figured that if patients were encouraged to think of something pleasurable, those thoughts could almost crowd out thoughts of pain. Mothers during delivery were encouraged to choose a focal point to concentrate on, maybe a song that was uplifting or a verse of Scripture. Children going through painful treatments were encouraged to think about a fun experience, something they looked forward to.

But long before anybody thought of a Gate Control Theory, the writer of Hebrews commended us to Jesus. He said that when we are running our race and we've hit the wall of suffering and trial, we should not look back, we should not look at our circumstances, but fix our eyes on Him. The fixing means that we don't look to the left or to the right. That will distract us. We don't look back. That will discourage us. We focus forward and lean into Him for strength. He showed us how to run the race of life. And He showed us how to finish well. He fixed His eyes on the joy that waited for Him on the other side of the cross. He gave His body to the nails, to the crown of thorns, to the spike

COUNT IT ALL JOY

in His side—knowing that victory and joy were waiting on the other side of His suffering. And I believe He says to us: *Go and do likewise.*

Stephen showed us how to do that. He was one of the first deacons of the church. And he was a bold witness for the gospel. As he defended the faith before the high priest and the Jews in Jerusalem, they were enraged and set about to stone him. But Stephen gazed into heaven—while he was being stoned—and saw the glory of God. "'Look,' he said, 'I see heaven open and the Son of Man standing at the right hand of God'" (Acts 7:56). He cried out to Jesus with his last breath, asking Him not to hold his attackers' sin against them. In his suffering he fixed his eyes on Jesus and found joy, unspeakable joy. Jesus who was seated at the right hand of the Father, was *standing* ready to welcome him home. He stood, and His standing gave strength to His suffering servant.

> **THE HARD TRUTH IS THAT FOR MANY OF US OUR SUFFERING AND TRIALS MAY NOT BE RESOLVED ON THIS SIDE OF HEAVEN.**

The hard truth is that for many of us our suffering and trials may not be resolved on this side of heaven. You may have received a depressing report from the doctor informing you that you only have months to live. You may be struggling with a long-term illness that there is no cure for. You may be held in a prison, awaiting certain death, in a country where it's unlawful to speak of Jesus. The writer of Hebrews would encourage us to fix our gaze forward on Jesus. Not on our circumstances. Not on our struggles. Just on Jesus.

DON'T GET WEARY

Knowing how hard it is to stay encouraged, the writer of Hebrews urges us to "Consider him who endured such opposition from sinners, so that you will not grow weary and lose heart" (Heb. 12:3). Don't give up. Don't throw in the towel. In the moments when it's almost too hard to breathe, He will carry you. He will renew and restore your strength. There is no greater joy than to lay your head on His bosom and rest a peaceful rest. He will rock you and speak peace to your soul and life to your bones. Keep your eyes on Him.

When Bill Broadhurst was eighteen he had an aneurysm on the right side of his brain. It caused the left side of his body to be partially paralyzed. After ten years he was finally able to walk without a cane, though he still had a noticeable limp. He always wanted to be a runner, so he signed up for the Pepsi Challenge 10,000-meter race in Omaha, Nebraska. When the starter pistol sounded on that July morning in 1981, the runners were off and thirty minutes later the winner, Bill Rodgers, crossed the finish line. But after two hours and twenty minutes, Bill Broadhurst was still running. There was no one in sight, and his left side was numb. His body screamed with pain, but he was determined to finish. He held 1 Corinthians 9:27 in his heart, thinking of Paul's encouragement for believers to run with endurance. The sky was getting dark when he finally reached the finish line. The crowds were gone. The banners had been taken down. But he hobbled along and finally made it across the finish line. And from the shadows, Bill Rodgers the marathon winner, emerged, along with a group of friends. Rodgers took his gold medal from his own neck and placed it on Broadhurst, declaring him the winner.[2]

That had to be a moment of pure joy. Finally making it across the finish line and your hero welcoming you with open arms. My friend, it will be like that if we endure, through seasons of weariness and struggle. Jesus our Savior will welcome us across that final finish line.

In a message on this text, Spurgeon said, "The race of holiness and patience, while it demands our vigor, displays our weakness. We are compelled, even before we take a step in the running, to bow the knee, and cry unto the strong for strength."[3] So we rejoice in knowing that there is strength in Him that helps us run our race. The old Negro spiritual says: "Walk together children, don't you get weary. There's a great camp meeting in the Promised Land!" We don't give up because there is a great camp meeting in the sky. We don't give up because kingdom joy awaits us.

KINGDOM JOY AWAITS

The winners in the Olympic games in Paul's day would train hard, pushing themselves to the point of exhaustion to win a crown made of olive leaves. But we are running to win a crown that will not perish. It is eternal. I rejoice that at the end of it all, I shall wear a crown. That's a long, long way from poverty in Mississippi. I will walk streets of gold. That's a long way from the hot asphalt pavement on Robinson Street. I will be in the land of no more. No more tears. No more suffering. No more pain. Nothing but joy and the presence of my Lord! "Therefore, since we are receiving a kingdom that cannot be shaken, let us be thankful, and so worship God acceptably with reverence and awe" (Heb. 12:28).

Robert Louis Stevenson tells of a storm that caught a vessel off a rocky coast and threatened to drive it and its passengers to destruction. In the midst of the terror, one daring man, contrary to orders, went to the deck, made a dangerous passage to the pilot house and saw the steer man, at his post holding the wheel unwaveringly, and inch by inch, turning the ship out, once more, to sea. The pilot saw the watcher and smiled. Then, the daring passenger went below and gave out a note of cheer: "I have seen the face of the pilot, and he smiled. All is well."[4]

Maybe your boat is struggling to make it into that shore of final rest. The winds are in your face and every day is harder than the last one. You're tired and you've run out of steam. Don't give up. Don't despair. You have a Pilot and a Finisher who knows how to get you there. I believe if we could see His face we would see His smile. No looks of concern or worry. He is in control of our lives. He has never lost a passenger. He will get you home, where there is no more suffering. Home where there is no more struggling. Home. Safe at last. Done with the troubles of this world.

Home. I think about that a lot. I used to be afraid to think about it. But now, it soothes my heart. Jesus, the author and finisher of my faith, is there. I think about all the saints of old He has brought safely into harbor. He is a Finisher who knows how to get you there. I trust in that truth. I rejoice in that truth. It will be glory to finally see Him. It will be inexpressible joy to finally see my Savior!

The hymn writer said it best:

Oh, I want to see Him, look upon His face,
There to sing forever of His saving grace;
On the streets of glory let me lift my voice,
Cares all past, home at last, ever to rejoice.[5]

Oh, I want to see Him! That will be JOY!

Even in the Valley of the Shadow of Death

I'm grateful to have been able to say what was on my heart. Pain and suffering are a part of this journey. He uses it to call us to repentance and to grow us up in our faith. He puts some stuff on us that's hard to bear so that we realize just how much we need Him. And He calls us to take on suffering for the good of others. My prayer is that you will not sit on the sidelines and watch people hurt, whether the hurting is from poverty, or from racism, or from bad choices. But that you will enter in to the suffering, share the pain, and bring healing and restoration. There's a world of hurting people who need that, especially now.

As I write this closing chapter, a new kind of suffering has invaded our land. It's something that I never expected to see in my lifetime. We are reeling from the deep, deep pain of political unrest as mobs of people have overrun our nation's Capitol building to prevent the certification of the election of our new president. Five persons have lost their lives, another one has committed suicide, and violence is threatened all over this land. The one word that I can't get out of my mind when I look at all of this is: *deception*. Many have been deceived and led astray to believe lies. It has become like a cancer in the soul of America. Just like the cancer that threatens to end my life at any moment, this cancer will destroy us if we do not radically remove it. The church must rise up and own our part in this great deception. Leaders of the evangelical church must speak boldly, bringing the healing balm of confession, truth, and righteousness to bear—while there is still time. We are guardians of truth, and we dare not neglect so great a call to courage of conviction. History will record the truth of whether we rose to the occasion at this crucial moment in time.

When I went into the hospital for surgery for my cancer, there were no guarantees that I would survive. No guarantees that I would live long enough to complete this book. The doctors gave me little time. But God in heaven has kept me and allowed me to finish what I want to call my manifesto. These last three books—*One Blood: Parting Words to the Church on Race and Love*, *He Calls Me Friend: The Healing Power of Friendship*, and *Count It All Joy: The Ridiculous Paradox of Suffering*—are the sum of the incarnational truths that He has taught me in my life. This is what I've learned from knowing this awesome God; this is the reality of the war we fought to the end. Yes, we fought to the very end and found joy in that place. These messages are a witness of how I believe we should live in a world that is fractured by racism, bigotry, strife, and so much pain. I want more than anything to encourage others to know that you can live a life of sacrifice, loving your enemies, doing good, and suffering for His name. And at the end of it all He promises paradoxical, inexpressible joy.

So, my friend, I count it all joy! I'm living at the doorway of heaven at ninety, aware that any day could be my last. I have my own physical suffering that I'm still dealing with, but joy is all around me. My heart overflows with gratitude for this joy. It has not diminished over time.

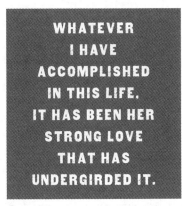

WHATEVER I HAVE ACCOMPLISHED IN THIS LIFE, IT HAS BEEN HER STRONG LOVE THAT HAS UNDERGIRDED IT.

It grows more radiant each and every day, with the promise of heaven set before me. My joy is finishing well; and my joy is that Vera Mae is still here with me, after seventy-one and a half years. She is feeble but in no pain. She has been such a part of me. You don't realize how much a person means to you until you almost lose them. God has kept her here and her presence has given me great strength. Whatever I have accomplished in this life, it has been her strong love that has undergirded it.

I wait for her to wake up every morning to spend time with her, to share with her what I've been learning from the Word. She listens and smiles back at me. I know that any morning when I go into her room I may find that she has gone home. My greatest joy would be to be able to lay her to rest and to follow close behind her. It would be the fulfillment of my promise to her grandmother that I would always take care of her. I even think of being able to hold her hand around the throne of heaven. One of my friends reminded me that I need to get my theology right. There is no marriage in heaven, but what we will have is even better. What a joy that will be!

That joy will only be multiplied when I am finally able to see my mother. I talk a lot about her, but I can't get away from the fact that she gave her life for me to live. And she suffered greatly before finally passing away. But she waits for me in that land of no more. She won't be impressed by honorary doctorates. She'll only want to know what I've done for people like her. I want to rush into her arms and tell her, "Momma, I did it! I spent my life working for poor people . . . for people like us." And I dream of hearing her say, "Well done, son. Well done." Oh, that will be joy.

> I WANT TO RUSH INTO HER ARMS AND TELL HER, "MOMMA, I DID IT! I SPENT MY LIFE WORKING FOR POOR PEOPLE . . . FOR PEOPLE LIKE US."

I read Ephesians 1:10–11 this morning and was reminded that we will soon be gathered together in Christ and we will be with Him for eternity. We were made for eternity. The pain and suffering in this life are how He gets us ready. I had been working for meaning to get glory for myself, but no more. In the days that remain I am working for that crown that I will lay at His feet. It took this pain and suffering to help me see that. This God gets us there. He is the Hound of Heaven who runs His prey down and gets us there. He is the Good Shepherd . . . He is my Shepherd.

> The Lord has been, and is my Shepherd
> I've not been in need.
> He maketh me to lie down in green pastures.
> He leadeth me beside the still water.
> And when Spencer and Wayne, my sons, died, He restored my soul.

He leadeth me in the path of righteousness
For His name's sake.
I don't have any of my own righteousness
He has put on us His clothes of righteousness.
I stand as if I never sinned.

Even as I walk through the valley of the shadow of death,
I will fear no evil, for you are with me.
Your rod, your staff, they comfort me.
You prepare a table before me—
that's the most precious time in life, when we can share a
common meal together.

You prepared a table before me
In the presence of my enemies.
I invited them in. I invited my enemies in.

Goodness and mercy, as I look back now, have followed me
all the days of my life.
They're gonna catch up with me soon.
I ought to have no fear because when grace and mercy
catch up with me.
They'll carry me into the house of the Lord forever.

My heart overflows with gratitude to my Savior for all of my journey. For keeping me till this very day. For allowing my Vera Mae to walk with me along the way. I am grateful. I'm almost there. I can almost see His face. I Count It All Joy!

Pure . . . paradoxical joy!

I read this book, *Count It All Joy*, through tears. It is very likely the last book John Perkins will ever write. It is possible that by the time you read this, he will have gone to glory with God. But he's leaving us with yet one more precious gift. It is as if he has summoned us all to his room to offer a benediction in the form of a mediation on suffering well. So, I wept and I listened. And I listened and I wept.

I first met John Perkins in the early 2010s. I had recently moved to Jackson, Mississippi, to get my master of divinity degree from a local seminary. As I was getting to know the city, I heard mention of this man, John Perkins. I noted that whenever someone spoke of him it was in reverent terms. You can tell a lot about a person's life and character by the way folks talk about them when they're not there. What I learned about Dr. Perkins even before I met him is that he is a man of integrity, compassion, faithfulness, and long-suffering.

The first time I had the opportunity to sit down in person with Dr. Perkins it was to discuss planting a church. I was a pastoral intern at a congregation nearby, and we were thinking about starting a new congregation in another part of the city. It would be intentionally multiracial, but also purposely located in an area of Jackson that had suffered from financial disinvestment. I remember he was so encouraging. I was a nobody, surprised he even agreed to meet with me. Yet he told me in that meeting, "It's a work that has to be done. And you can do it. You can do it."

God had other plans, and I ended up starting a nonprofit organization, but I never forgot the sincerity and intensity of his voice when he blessed me with his confidence in me.

Dr. Perkins learned love through suffering. He was born into struggle in 1930 during the Great Depression. He wasn't just born anyplace, either. His birthplace was Mississippi, the stronghold of the Jim Crow South. He was only able to attain a third-grade education in terms of formal schooling because his family labored under the oppressive burden of poverty. His mother died of pellagra—a niacin deficiency due to malnutrition—when he was just seven months old. His father left, and his grandparents raised him. The tragedies in Dr. Perkins's life continued to pile up like bricks being piled onto someone's back—a brutal beating in a rural Mississippi jail, the early deaths of two children, bouts with cancer, and the daily struggle for good in a callous world. Under these burdens, his knees could have buckled, and he could have collapsed at any moment. But through faith in God and the support of family and friends, he found a way to press forward.

Because of his lifetime of faithful struggle, John Perkins's name is synonymous with justice. He cofounded the Christian Community Development Association in 1989 to pursue holistic change—both spiritual and material. His efforts made him an international speaker and earned him more than a dozen honorary degrees from various colleges and universities. In 2004, Seattle Pacific University founded the John Perkins Center for Reconciliation, Leadership Training, and Community Development. In 2012, Calvin University established the John M. Perkins Leadership Fellows "to address big issues like poverty, injustice, racism and materialism."[1] Dr. Perkins's vision for restoration and action through service continues on through the young people in these programs.

In *Count It All Joy*, John Perkins addresses the ancient and vexing questions—Why do we suffer, and how do we suffer well? To answer the question, he goes back to his old mainstay—the Bible. James 1:2–4 reads, "Count it all joy, my brothers, when you meet trials of various kinds, for you know that the testing of your faith produces steadfastness. And let steadfastness have its full effect, that you may be perfect and complete, lacking in nothing" (ESV). This isn't a passage that is popular among anyone, least of all social justice activists. People who are fighting for justice don't want to hear that suffering has some bigger purpose. They want to make it clear that injustice—racism, poverty, xenophobia, misogyny, and the like—are forms of suffering that should not be present in the first place. But Dr. Perkins reminds us that suffering molds us into people who can both work to reshape the world and our own souls into something better and more loving.

Dr. Perkins makes clear that God uses suffering—that which is imposed on us and that which we choose for the sake of the gospel—to turn our eyes toward Jesus. When we behold the face of Jesus during our trials, we get more than strength, more than fortitude; we get joy. As Perkins says, "Only God can put suffering together with joy and make it make sense." This is an inscrutable paradox, that the deepest darkness would reveal the light. It would hardly be believable unless a man like John Perkins, with all his scars and battle wounds in the struggle for justice, was telling us.

I needed this book. Dr. Perkins's words met me in a time of suffering in my life. I read the book near Mother's Day. It was the first Mother's Day since my own mother had died a few months earlier. Just after her death, a friend told me that grief comes in waves and at unexpected times. I wasn't expecting the sadness and even anger on that Sunday as I saw so many others gushing about their mothers and smiling in pictures with them. I was also feeling the acute sense of being harassed. As a public critic of racism and a proponent of racial justice, I don't know if I'll ever get used to going online and seeing that yet another person has labeled and libeled me. Although the work is good, it is wearying.

Count It All Joy tells us that God sees us. Whatever you're going through right now, Dr. Perkins sagely advises, "You can take all that pain to Him. He is waiting for you. He hears your faintest cry. He will hold you. He will keep you. I beg you to trust Him." John Perkins's life, even on the brink of death, is a testimony that God is with us in the middle of our agonies.

We are living in the final days of the generation that lived through the Civil Rights movement. Soon they will all pass away. As a historian, this fact grieves me. All that wisdom, all those experiences will quickly be accessible only in what these women and men left behind. As a black Christian, I am afflicted with despondence because men like John Perkins are the witnesses I look to for guidance. In many ways, we still need their living witness to help us navigate the rocks of racism, the potholes of prejudice, and the uncertainties of the Christian life. My heart cries, "Don't leave us! Not yet."

As I think of a world where John Perkins is a memory, I weep. Men of his faith, vigor, and tenacity are rare. He has been working for justice, reconciliation, and peace with God for longer than most of us have been alive. "As I am closing in on the final chapter of my life, I see things clearer than I did before," he wrote. I am glad for his clarity. I must confess, though, that as Dr.

Perkins nears the end of this phase of his existence, I can hardly see a thing through the midst of my tears.

Each generation will have to find their own way. We cannot live in the past nor can we replicate it. That's not what John Perkins would want us to do anyway. He wants us to learn from him, yes, from his mistakes, but also from his suffering. But he does not leave us to figure it out all on our own. He has left us the words in this book as a lamp to illuminate our steps.

We should pay careful attention to parting words. Jesus' last words before He ascended into heaven were, "But you will receive power when the Holy Spirit has come upon you, and you will be my witnesses in Jerusalem and in all Judea and Samaria, and to the end of the earth" (Acts 1:8 ESV). John Perkins heeded those words and bore witness to the power of Jesus Christ to transform hearts, minds, and conditions for the glory of God. Now, in order to offer our own witness to this generation and those that follow, we should listen to John Perkins's parting words . . . "count it all joy."

JEMAR TISBY
New York Times bestselling author, *The Color of Compromise*;
Assistant Director, The Center for Antiracist Research at Boston University

CHAPTER ONE: CHOSEN TO SUFFER

1. Do you believe that if you are good you can avoid suffering? How does our culture reinforce this message, and how does the story of Job challenge that kind of thinking?

2. How difficult is it for you to look beyond and through your suffering to see what God is trying to accomplish in your life?

3. How does saying, "You'll get over it," to someone who is suffering do damage rather than encourage?

CHAPTER TWO: THE UNANSWERABLE "WHY"

1. Talk about the times in your life when you have found yourself asking God, "Why?"

2. Why is lament so important; where are the safe places for you to lament? If you've not found that place, consider writing out your lament to God.

3. Helen Roseveare came to see her deep suffering as a privilege. In what way can your present suffering be seen as a privilege?

CHAPTER THREE: TESTED BY SUFFERING

1. Dr. Perkins says that while God is testing us, Satan is wooing us in one of three ways: the lust of the flesh, the lust of the eyes, or the pride of life. How is the enemy wooing you?

2. As you suffer do you find yourself being tested most in the area of patience or gentleness? Talk about how this displays itself in your life.

3. How have your family and friends been tested by your suffering?

CHAPTER FOUR: I SEE HIM

1. How has your suffering caused you to question or be assured of the goodness of God?

2. Discuss how you have been strengthened by each of these attributes of God amid suffering: sovereignty, omnipotence, omnipresence.

3. Dr. Perkins suggests that suffering not only helps us see God rightly, but it also helps us see ourselves. How has the Lord used your suffering to reveal your true heart?

CHAPTER FIVE: THE CASE FOR SUFFERING

1. How have you taken on suffering for the advance of the gospel in your own life?

2. Most of Dr. Perkins's life has been spent suffering for the cause of justice. What commitments have you made personally?

3. God uses our own brokenness to prepare us to serve those who suffer in similar ways. How has He uniquely prepared you as a sufferer?

CHAPTER SIX: IN HIS STEPS

1. How might your life change if you made a commitment to ask "what would Jesus do" before every decision?

2. In the Sermon on the Mount Jesus taught us what it looks like to serve Him, and often to suffer for Him, in a dark world. Which of the sayings is the most difficult for you? Why?

3. A hallmark of the life of a believer, and certainly of Dr. Perkins's life, is the choice to forgive those who hurt us. How have you been challenged to display this characteristic as a sufferer?

CHAPTER SEVEN: DEAL WITH FEAR

1. We have a choice as believers, to suffer or to take the easy road. What choice have you made? Explain the factors that influenced this choice.

2. How has fear crippled you in responding to the needs of others? How have you chosen to address fear in your own heart?

3. The COVID pandemic provided a treasure trove of opportunities for us to give sacrificially and put the needs of others ahead of our own. How did the Lord prompt you to enter into the suffering of others during this time?

CHAPTER EIGHT: HE CAN REDEEM IT ALL!

1. How has the Lord used suffering in your life to drive the roots of your faith deeper in Him?

2. We are encouraged and strengthened by the testimonies of Bible heroes and other faithful believers. Their example spurs us on. How has God used your endurance to impact the lives of those around you?

3. Dr. Perkins's calling to the ministry of social justice came through the death of his son. God uses suffering to birth new ministries and new callings in our lives. How might He be calling you to new ministry through your suffering?

CHAPTER NINE: MY EYES ARE FIXED

1. The Gate Control Theory argues that if we fix our eyes/minds on something desirable it can minimize the effect of pain. What do you fix your mind on when suffering is the most difficult?

2. It's human to get tired. Dr. Perkins has spoken often of the weariness of life. How do you fight against the urge to just quit?

3. Whether we suffer because we have been chosen to suffer, or whether we willingly choose to suffer with others— joy awaits us. Talk about that joy. How can you keep this truth in the forefront of your mind along your journey?

ACKNOWLEDGMENTS

Every day I have the opportunity through Zoom and my writing to connect with sisters and brothers around the globe who say they are following my example in suffering for the cause of Christian community development. These precious souls have now become my teachers, applying the principles we hammered out during and after the difficult days of the civil rights movement in new ways fit for this millennium. I simply must give thanks for the privilege of being a part of this movement.

Leaders are important, but movements require followers. I pay homage to those who followed Vera Mae and me into hard and difficult places for the sake of the gospel.

First and foremost are my children, who, though they really had no choice, suffered in ways that I have only discovered in recent years. They could not reveal their sufferings for fear of burdening us as we faced the fires of the fight for civil rights. But they always stood with us, and have loved us even though they have often had to take second place to our work, our ministry, and our calling, at great personal cost to themselves. I simply say to you, my beloved, "I love you, I beg your forgiveness, and I long for the day when we will all be in that place of peace that is forever."

In addition to my birth children, I find it in my heart to express my deepest respect and gratitude to our firstborn children in ministry, Rev. Artis and Carolyn Fletcher and Rev. Dr. Dolphus and Rosie Weary. It is not an overstatement to say that had it not been for these two couples—coming to faith in Christ in our struggling ministry in Mendenhall in the 1960s, leaving Mississippi to receive their educations in the promised land of California, and then returning to rural Mississippi to expand the work beyond anything Vera Mae and I could have ever conceived—none of what others generously attribute to our lives would have ever taken place.

And beyond our birth children, and our firstborn by faith, there came another group of adopted children. Ervin and Joan Huston and H and Terry Spees were among the first white sisters and brothers to come not to visit but to live, to join their lives, to leave their homes and make our ministry their home. Their willingness to struggle with us put flesh on the vision of a multicultural gospel that could burn through white supremacy and lift blacks out of inferiority to the gospel of forgiveness. This is where our human dignity is affirmed. This is the model for gospel reconciliation that is at the heart of Jesus' strategy for redeeming individuals and communities.

My dear friend Wayne Gordon and his wife, Ann, took this vital message to the city of Chicago, to the continent of Africa, and around the world. Beyond these seed planters, there have been hundreds and thousands more—remainers, returners, and relocators—whose lives form a panoramic video of memories and transformational outcomes. I don't dare name a single one of you for fear of leaving one precious friend and partner out. You know who you are. You know the love and the pain we have shared and faced together. Without you, I would be nothing. With you, my joy is complete.

And finally, my deepest appreciation and gratitude is extended to Moody Publishers, Duane Sherman, and Karen

Waddles, who saw the vision for these three books that I call my manifesto. May our Lord make much of the work of our hands for His awesome glory.

NOTES

FOREWORD

1. John M. Perkins, *Dream with Me: Race, Love, and the Struggle We Must Win* (Grand Rapids: Baker, 2017), 79.
2. John M. Perkins with Karen Waddles, *One Blood: Parting Words to the Church on Race and Love* (Chicago: Moody, 2018), 171.

INTRODUCTION

1. See "Sending Up My Timber lyrics," AllTheLyrics.com, https://www .allthelyrics com/lyrics/gospel/sending_up_my_timber-lyrics-1155575.html.
2. Henry Cloud and John Townsend, *How People Grow: What the Bible Reveals about Personal Growth* (Grand Rapids: Zondervan, 2001), 150.
3. John Perkins, *One Blood: Parting Words to the Church on Race and Love* (Chicago: Moody, 2018), 174.
4. Arthur Bennett, *The Valley of Vision* (Edinburgh, UK: The Banner of Truth Trust, 1975), 22.
5. Dr. Martin Luther King Jr., Speech at Grosse Point Historical Society, March 14, 1968, https://www.gphistorical.org/mlk/mlkspeech/mlkaudio.htm.
6. "Twelfth Night," Literary Devices, https://literarydevices.net/twelfth-night/.
7. "No Wayz Tired" (aka I Don't Feel Noways Tired) by Curtis Burrell Copyright (c) 1977 by Peermusic III, Ltd. and Savgos Music, Inc. Administered by Peermusic III, Ltd. on behalf of itself and Savgos Music, Inc. All Rights Reserved. Used By Permission.
8. Pamela Rose Williams, "Top 15 Christian Quotes about Pain and Suffering," https://www.whatchristianswanttoknow.com/top-15-christian-quotes-about-pain-and-suffering/.

PRELUDE

1. Franklin D. Roosevelt, Inaugural Address, March 4, 1933, as published in Samuel Rosenman, ed., *The Public Papers of Franklin D. Roosevelt, Volume Two: The Year of Crisis, 1933* (New York: Random House, 1938), 11–16, http://historymatters.gmu.edu/d/5057/.

2. Ibid.

3. Mark Dance, "The Battle of Gethsemane," https://markdance.net/the-battle-of-gethsemane/.

4. J. I. Packer, *Knowing God,* quoted in Charles R. Swindoll, *The Tale of the Tardy Oxcart* (Nashville: Word Publishing, 1998), 236.

5. "John of the Cross: Purifying the Soul," in *Devotional Classics,* revised and expanded, Richard J. Foster and James Bryan Smith, eds. (San Francisco: HarperSanFrancisco, 2005), 37; quoted in John Ortberg, *Soul Keeping: Caring for the Most Important Part of You* (Grand Rapids: Zondervan, 2014), 182–83.

CHAPTER ONE: CHOSEN TO SUFFER

1. Eugene J. Mayhew, "Job," in *The Moody Bible Commentary,* Michael Rydelnik and Michael Vanlaningham, eds. (Chicago: Moody, 2014), 697.

2. Francis Andersen, *Job: An Introduction and Commentary* (Downers Grove, IL: InterVarsity Press, 1976), 88.

3. Paul David Tripp, *Suffering: Gospel Hope When Life Doesn't Make Sense* (Wheaton, IL: Crossway, 2018), 176.

4. Thomas Brookes, *The Mute Christian Under the Smarting Rod,* quoted in (Nashville: Word Publishing, 1998), Charles Swindoll, *The Tale of the Tardy Oxcart,* 585.

5. Tripp, *Suffering,* 150.

6. A. W. Tozer, *The Root of the Righteous,* quoted in Greg Herrick, "Consider it All Joy," https://bible.org/article/consider-it-all-joy.

CHAPTER TWO: THE UNANSWERABLE "WHY"

1. Abdi Latif Dahir, "Instead of Coronavirus, the Hunger Will Kill Us. A Global Food Crisis Looms," *The New York Times,* April 22, 2020, https://www.nytimes.com/2020/04/22/world/africa/coronavirus-hunger-crisis.html.

2. Mark Vroegop, *Weep with Me: How Lament Opens a Door for Reconciliation* (Wheaton, IL: Crossway, 2020), 37.

3. K. J. Ramsey, *This Too Shall Last: Finding Grace When Suffering Lingers* (Grand Rapids: Zondervan, 2020), 158.

4. Helen Roseveare, quoted in Charles Swindoll, *The Tale of the Tardy Oxcart,* (Nashville: Word Publishing, 1998), 245.

CHAPTER THREE: TESTED BY SUFFERING

1. **Through It All**, Andrae E. Crouch © Copyright 1971, Renewed 1999. Manna Music, Inc./ASCAP (admin. By ClearBox Rights). All rights reserved. Used by permission.
2. Neil T. Anderson, *The Bondage Breaker* (Eugene, OR: Harvest House Publishers, 2000), 142.
3. *Hupomeno*, Thayer's Greek Lexicon, "Greek/Hebrew Definitions," https://www.bibletools.org/index.cfm/fuseaction/Lexicon.show/ID/G5278/hupomeno.htm.
4. James S. Hewitt, *Illustrations Unlimited*, quoted in Charles Swindoll, *The Tale of the Tardy Oxcart*, (Nashville: Word Publishing, 1998), 67.
5. Nancy DeMoss Wolgemuth, "The Way Up Is Down," adapted from *Brokenness: the Heart God Revives* (Chicago: Moody, 2002), https://www.reviveourhearts.com/articles/the-way-up-is-down/.

CHAPTER FOUR: I SEE HIM

1. Kelly Rosati, "Kay Warren: Moms of Kids with Illness Need Christ and Community," *Christianity Today*, Nov. 12, 2019, https://www.christianitytoday.com/ct/2019/november-web-only/kay-warren-moms-kids-mental-illness-need-christ-community.html.
2. Ray Pritchard, *Keep Believing* (Chicago: Moody, 1997), 41–42.
3. Charles Ryrie, *Basic Theology* (Chicago: Moody, 1999), 46.
4. Dietrich Bonhoeffer, *Life Together: The Classic Exploration of Christian Community* (New York: HarperCollins, 1954), 110.
5. "Hymn Stories: Rock of Ages," https://reasonabletheology.org/hymn-stories-rock-of-ages-cleft-for-me/.
6. Dave Furman, *Kiss the Wave: Embracing God in Our Trials* (Wheaton, IL: Crossway, 2018), 18.

CHAPTER FIVE: THE CASE FOR SUFFERING

1. Ignatius, "The Epistle of Ignatius to the Romans," https://www.catholica.com/epistle-of-ignatius-to-the-romans/.
2. David Anderson, "Praying on the Armor of God," May 2007, https://www.facebook.com/AndersonSpeaks/photos/pray-on-the-armor-of/663846103819819/.
3. "History of Mission: Lott Carey," based on excerpts from *Lott Carey, First Black Missionary to Africa*, by Leroy Fitts (Valley Forge, PA: Judson

Press, 1978), http://www.thetravelingteam.org/articles/lott-carey.

4. Lott Cary, quoted in Miles Mark Fisher, "Lott Cary, the Colonizing Missionary," *Journal of Negro History* 7, no. 4 (October 1922): https://www.journals.uchicago.edu/doi/pdfplus/10.2307/2713721.

5. Providence Baptist Church website, http://www.providencebc.net/history/.

6. Marvin Newell, *A Martyr's Grace: Stories of Those Who Gave All For Christ and His Cause* (Chicago: Moody, 2006), 21.

7. Ibid., 20.

8. Eric Mason, *Woke Church: An Urgent Call for Christians in America to Confront Racism and Injustice* (Chicago: Moody, 2018), 55.

9. Roz Edward, "Congressman John Lewis Dies at the Age of 80," *Atlanta Tribune*, July 20, 2020, https://atlantatribune.com/2020/07/20/congressman-john-lewis-dies-at-the-age-of-80/.

10. "Fannie Lou Hamer," Biography, February 10, 2018, updated June 19, 2020, https://www.biography.com/activist/fannie-lou-hamer.

11. Donna Britt, "A White Mother Went to Alabama to Fight for Civil Rights. The Klan Killed Her for It.," *Washington Post*, December 15, 2017, https://www.washingtonpost.com/news/retropolis/wp/2017/12/15/a-white-mother-went-to-alabama-to-fight-for-civil-rights-the-klan-killed-her-for-it/.

12. Ibid.

13. John Perkins, *A Quiet Revolution* (Pasadena, CA: Urban Family Publications, 1976), 16–17.

14. C. S. Lewis, *The Problem of Pain* (New York: Macmillan, 1961), 98.

15. Kelly Rosati, "Kay Warren: Moms of Kids with Mental Illness Need Christ and Community," *Christianity Today*, November, 2019, https://www.christianitytoday.com/ct/2019/november-web-only/kay-warren-moms-kids-mental-illness-need-christ-community.html.

16. J. L. Wilson, *Pastoral Ministry in the Real World: Loving, Teaching, and Leading God's People* (Bellingham, WA: Lexham Press, 2016), 38–41.

17. Robert Kelleman, *Spiritual Friends: A Methodology of Soul Care and Spiritual Direction* (Taneytown, MD: RPM Books, 2005), 49.

18. Paul David Tripp, *Suffering: Gospel Hope When Life Doesn't Make Sense* (Wheaton, IL: Crossway, 2018), 200.

CHAPTER SIX: IN HIS STEPS

1. Charles Sheldon, *In His Steps* (Grand Rapids: Baker Publishing, 1984).
2. Louis Barbieri, "1 Peter," in *The Moody Bible Commentary*, Michael Rydelnik and Michael Vanlaningham, eds. (Chicago: Moody, 2014), 1957.
3. Vance Havner, Sermon Illustrations, Sermon Central, https://www .sermoncentral.com/sermon-illustrations/61801/vance-havner-said-at-the-nicene-council-an-by-sermon-central.
4. Henri J. M. Nouwen, *The Way of the Heart: Desert Spirituality and Contemporary Ministry* (San Francisco: HarperSanFrancisco, 1981), 34.
5. C. S. Lewis, *The C. S. Lewis Signature Classics* (New York: HarperCollins, 2017), 77.
6. "Giving," Chaplain Magazine, http://www.sermonillustrations.com/ a-z/g/giving.htm.
7. Stephen E. Berk, *A Time to Heal: John Perkins, Community Development, and Racial Reconciliation* (Grand Rapids: Baker Books, 1997), 186.
8. Dr. Martin Luther King Jr., Speech at Grosse Point Historical Society, March 14, 1968, https://www.gphistorical.org/mlk/mlkspeech/mlkaudio .htm.
9. David Key, "Would You Change Your Nature?," Lake Oconee Breeze newsletter, May 21, 2015, https://www.lakeoconeebreeze.net/opinion/ columns/would-you-change-your-nature/article_b70eb5b0-ffed-11e4-94df-6f3956180a94.html.

CHAPTER SEVEN: DEAL WITH FEAR

1. Kate Shellnut, "2020's Most-Read Bible Verse," *Christianity Today*, December 3, 2020, https://www.christianitytoday.com/news/2020/ december/most-popular-verse-youversion-app-bible-gateway-fear-covid .html.
2. John M. Perkins, *Dream with Me* (Grand Rapids: Baker Books, 2017), 37.
3. John Piper, "Fear Not, I Am With You, I Am Your God," June 20, 1993, https://www.desiringgod.org/messages/fear-not-i-am-with-you-i-am-your-god.
4. Maurice Dubois, "Five Years Later Subway Hero Is Still the Man," CBS New York Online, Feb. 21, 2012, https://newyork.cbslocal.com/2012/02/21/ 5-years-later-new-york-city-subway-hero-wesley-autrey-is-still-the-man/.

CHAPTER EIGHT: HE CAN REDEEM IT ALL!

1. "Please Be Patient With Me" by Sim Wilson Copyright (c) 1979 by Peermusic III, Ltd. and Savgos Music, Inc. Administered by Peermusic III, Ltd. on behalf of itself and Savgos Music, Inc. All Rights Reserved. Used By Permission.
2. Our Daily Bread, "Deep Roots," https://bible.org/illustration/deep-roots.
3. Berit Kjos, *A Wardrobe from the King* (Wheaton, IL: Victor Books, 1988), 45–46, found in http://www.sermonillustrations.com/a-z/p/peace.htm.
4. Monica Dickens, *Miracles of Courage*, 1985, found in https://bible.org/illustration/thank-you-my-hurting.

CHAPTER NINE: MY EYES ARE FIXED

1. Joel Katz and Brittany N. Rosenbloom, "Golden Anniversary of Melzack and Wall's Gate Control Theory of Pain: Celebrating 50 Years of Pain Research and Management," *Pain Research & Management* 20, no. 6 (November–December 2015): 285–86, https://www.ncbi.nlm.nih.gov/pmc/articles/PMC4676495/.
2. R. Kent Hughes, "The Key to True Grit," www.crossway.org/articles/the-key-to-true-grit/.
3. C. H. Spurgeon, "The Rule of the Race," in *The Metropolitan Tabernacle Pulpit Sermons*, vol. 34 (London: Passmore & Alabaster, 1888), 434.
4. Source unknown, "He Smiled," Sermon Illustrations, https://bible.org/illustration/he-smiled.
5. Rufus H. Cornelius, "Oh, I Want to See Him," Timeless Truths, 1916, https://library.timelesstruths.org/music/Oh_I_Want_to_See_Him/.

AFTERWORD

1. "John M. Perkins Leadership Fellows," Calvin University, https://calvin.edu/leadership-fellows/.

JOHN M. PERKINS

Dr. John M. Perkins is cofounder of the Christian Community Development Association, and founder and president emeritus of the John and Vera Mae Perkins Foundation for Reconciliation, Justice, and Christian Community Development in Jackson, Mississippi. An internationally known speaker and activist, advisor to five US presidents, he is the author of many books, including *Let Justice Roll Down*, named by *Christianity Today* as one of the top fifty books that have shaped evangelicals.

KAREN L. WADDLES

Karen Waddles is a graduate of DePaul University and is completing a MASF at Moody Theological Seminary. She is a coauthor for John Perkins's *One Blood* and *He Calls Me Friend*; and a contributing writer for *Our Voices: Issues Facing Black Women in America* (Moody Publishers), the *Women of Color Study Bible* (Nia Publishing), and the *Sisters in Faith Devotional Bible* (Thomas Nelson).

Civil Rights Legend

Counselor to Five Presidents

Community Development Lead

Learn more about
the life, legacy and manifesto of John M. Perkins at

johnmperkins.com